THE SOCIO-ECONOMIC STATUS TRENDS OF THE

MEXICAN PEOPLE RESIDING IN ARIZONA

A Thesis

Arizona State College

At Tempe

By

Raymond Johnson Flores, A. B.

1951

Reprinted in 1973 by

R AND E RESEARCH ASSOCIATES

4843 Mission St., San Francisco 94112

18581 McFarland Ave., Saratoga, CA 95070

Publishers and Distributors of Ethnic Studies

Editor: Adam S. Eterovich

Publisher: Robert D. Reed

Library of Congress Card Catalog Number

73-76009

ISBN

0-88247-211-9

"The one thing every individual <u>must</u> do is to live; the one thing
that society <u>must</u> do is to secure from each individual his fair contribution
to the general well being and see to it that a just return is made to him."

- - - John Dewey

FOREWORD

This thesis was about the largest minority group in Arizona, the Mexicans, generous, warmhearted seekers of social equality and of economic security yet exploited, segregated and submerged. In Arizona they numbered around 100,000 persons. A few were the descendants of early Spanish colonials, some came as a result of the Mexican Revolution in 1910, others came because they sought to improve their own standards of living, and a few had arrived in the last few years. They were employed in the state's agricultural and mining industries, in the unskilled trades, in the skilled crafts, as small shopkeepers, in private enterprise, and a small number were active in the professional fields. Their homes were found to be located in distinctive areas; while some were living in mixed Anglo-American and Mexican-American areas, generally their homes were to be found in the clustered areas that made up the slum sections of Phoenix, Tucson, and other low-rent districts throughout the state. They have suffered injustice and discrimination in their economic, social, cultural and political life. Culturally, they have retained many characteristics that, due to the proximity of the Mexican border and its influence, have hindered the process of Americanization for the group.

The most serious handicap encountered in the preparation of this thesis was the lack of reliable material and the meagerness of available statistics. The majority of Federal, state, and other agencies contacted had followed the United States Census practice which classified the Mexican as white. Labor organizations made no distinction as to nationality or race, merely classifying by skill or trade. The figures and material presented in this thesis were subject to limitations in that (1) all sources disagreed as to exactness of statistics; (2) the information presented herein was gathered through interviews and a survey questionnaire; and (3) as such, these data indicated trends and approximations only.

Among the many to whom this writer is indebted for making this study possible are: Dr. Irma Wilson, who gave of her time and encouragement in seeing this study carried out; Mrs. Placida G. Smith, of the Phoenix Friendly House, who gave of her time and assistance in surveying the Phoenix area; Mr. Raul Castro, attorney, who aided in the survey of the Tucson area and Miss Ida Price, who assisted in the proofreading of this study.

R.J.F.

TABLE OF CONTENTS

CHAPTER I

INTRODUCTION

I. THE GENERAL NATURE OF THE PROBLEM

The descendants of the Mexican and of the early Spanish colonials who immigrated to Arizona represented the largest minority group residing there. Numerically they represented around 26 per cent of the state's total white population. The Arizona group is a small segment of a larger group which is geographically concentrated in those Southwestern states having a common border with Mexico. Colorado, which had a large Mexican population, was the only state not bordering on Mexico. In the years following the first World War, and during the second World War, this large immigrant group has spread to the urban-industrial areas of the East, Midwest and West coast. In areas where they have formed colonies, they have tended to retain many of the cultural traits which distinguish them from other groups. Where they have become a part of the large impersonal city, they have adjusted readily to the dominant Anglo-American cultural patterns.

In Arizona the assimilation of this large minority group has been slow. The impedient factors have been primarily based on racial, socio-economic, political, national and religious misconceptions, which have been expressed through hatred and bigotry.

II. THE PROBLEM

Statement of the problem. It was the purpose of this study to ascertain the socio-economic status trends of the Mexican people of the state of Arizona. This study was based on a consideration of their social and economic status patterns as affected by (1) the constant and incessant social turmoil and (2) the economic factors which have contributed to their status.

Importance of this study. Human relations are today more than ever playing their greatest social role. The whole situation embraces all of man's world. Men, if they are to live and work together, must seek to understand one another. The fate of mankind depends largely on man's ability to reduce those tensions and practices which threaten the peace of families, communities, states and nations.

Because socio-economic status differences have produced, along with racial, national origin, and cultural misconceptions, strained relations between the Anglo-American and the Mexican-American people of this state, this study was undertaken to point out the underlying forces causing these strained relations and the underlying causes of the retarded socio-economic status of the Mexicans in Arizona. Moreover, it was the sincere desire of the researcher and his advisory staff that this work and these data provide a basis of understanding and information for those concerned with the improvement of inter-group relations in the state of Arizona.

III. DEFINITION OF TERMS USED

Mexican. The term "Mexican" as it was used in this study designates those Americans whose antecedents came from Mexico, or are of Mexican national origin. The term further includes those Americans who are descendants of the early Spanish colonials and their descendants. There was no readily identifiable homogeneous characteristic by which to identify them. They ranged in physical complexion characteristics from blonde to brunette, the greater number being somewhere between these two extremes. In this study, as in their community life, they have been referred to by such names as Mexican-Americans, Spanish-Americans, Spanish-speaking, Latin-Americans, and Spanish-name. The term "Spanish" designates either the nationality given or the language spoken. It was not unusual to find in the conducting of this study some who called themselves French-Mexicans or Irish-Mexicans, according to the admixture of their parental origin. The term "Mexican" was not used as a means of designating or differentiating any one grouping intentionally, but rather as a means of simplifying writing and tabular research. "Spanish-name" tabulations were used where no other possible identifiable characteristic existed.

Anglo-American. The term "Anglo" or "Anglo-American" as used in this study designates that numerically dominant segment of the total population of the Southwest which is not Mexican in national origin, and which, broadly speaking, has much the same culture in all regions of this nation.

Socio-economic status trends. As used in this study, the term "socio-economic status trends" was conceived as applying to the periodic fluctuations in the social and economic status of the Mexican people in the state of Arizona, with reference to average standards of cultural possessions, effective income, material possessions, social position, group acceptance, social ostracism, and community participation.

Cultural. As used in this study, the term "cultural" denotes the acquisitions of the group, i.e., music, religion, social customs, government, and education.

IV. SCOPE, METHOD AND APPROACH OF THE STUDY

Scope. The scope of this study was restricted to a consideration and presentation of the social and economic factors which affected the Mexican people of the state of Arizona.

Method. The methods of research used in this study consisted of two major types: (1) the historical and (2) the normative-survey. The techniques of collecting data were (1) documentary evidence, ie., census information, government publications, private agency reports, previous research studies; (2) the mailed questionnaire, for opinion and fact and (3) the interview, for opinion and fact.

Approach. Although this study was carried out under the supervision of the Foreign Language Department at Arizona State College, Tempe, the approach to this study was sociological.

V. A HISTORICAL DELINEATION

The role of the Mexicans in Arizona's development has been that of furnishing the manual labor required to build a mineral empire and make the earth produce.

Mexico and colonization. Mexico's colonization came during the early sixteenth century. Serving as a base of operations for the gold-searching conquistadores and for the heathen-seeking missionaries, Mexico was the crucible from which were to come the thousands of Mexicans that followed the mission roads north to the fabulous gold and silver mines of the northern Sonora desert. As the missions spread north, so went the people. Tucson, said to be one of the oldest settlements in the United States, was the northern outpost of the colonial Mexicans.

Territorial days. On February 2, 1848, as a result of the war between the United States and Mexico, Mexico ceded to the United States the territory that included all of what comprises California, New Mexico, Arizona, and other large fragments of land. This treaty, known as the Treaty of Guadalupe Hidalgo,[1] also granted the rights and privileges of American citizens to all citizens of Mexico residing within the ceded domain. Articles VIII and IX of the treaty[2] also stipulated that citizens of Mexico who did not signify their desire to retain their Mexican citizenship, within one year after ratification of the treaty, would be guaranteed property and political rights including the attempt at " . . . safeguarding their cultural autonomy, that is, they were given the right to retain their language, religion, and culture. "[3]

It was not officially known how many Mexicans took advantage of this opportunity for obtaining American citizenship, but there were some Mexican families living in Arizona who claimed to be descendants of settlers that came to Arizona in the pre-territorial and early territorial days.[4] The coming of the Mexican to Arizona had fulfilled the need for muscular strength to develop the mines in the southern section of the state.

Prior to statehood, and until 1924, the early Arizona Mexican population fluctuated constantly. These people would come and return across the territorial boundary with little or no restriction. Estimates as to their numbers had been made by the various writers in the field. The United States Censuses presented only figures representing the number of Mexican-born whites in the state of Arizona. All other figures given were mere estimates or approximations.

The Mexicans after 1912. During territorial days there was a great influx of Anglo-Americans who came to the western mine fields seeking wealth and adventure. Along the southern tier of counties could be found many Southerners who had left Texas and the South immediately after the end of the Civil War. In the northern parts of Arizona were families who had migrated west from the New England areas. Their coming brought to Arizona mineral and agricultural expansion that, in turn, created a further need for cheap labor. Mexico was their ready source of supply. The Mexicans arriving during those early days were, by and large, miners and agricultural workers. Their increasing numbers during the state's early period of expansion was a positive indication of the state's rapid growth.

The advent of the Anglo-American group introduced methods and a culture entirely foreign to the native Mexican population. The resultant clash of cultures produced many and varied problems for the two groups. The greatest problem was that of accommodation. The Mexican group, which had a culture less advanced than that of the Anglo group, soon found itself the victim of discriminatory pressures exerted by the rapidly growing Anglo-American group. As the gap widened, differences gave way to misconceptions. The word Mexican became synonymous with the term peon. This attitude had changed but slightly at the time of this investigation. In illustrating this attitude, Carey McWilliams state: "The ease and swiftness of the victory over Mexico and the conquest of California had bred in the American a measureless contempt for all things Mexican."[5] Another example of this attitude on the part of the Anglo-Americans, which had existed up until the second World War, was that attitude held by Silvester Mowry. Writing in 1864, Mowry state:

> The substitution of white for peon labor would be a failure, owing to the debilitating influence which the climate exerts on Northerners. The Mexican labor is good when properly superintended; but, to render it advantageous, the recognition of the traditionary custom of peonage is necessary.[6]

In the twenty-year period preceding the depression of the 1930-1940 period, the Mexicans received progressively better treatment than before. They were considered an essential "economic commodity", and there was a consequent increase in their wages. Salaries compared favorably with that of other unskilled workers; and as long as the Mexicans remained docile and did not react against untoward conditions, they were tolerated to a large extent in the public eating and recreational establishments. Rosalio Florian Munoz, writing on conditions in 1938, stated:

> The attitude toward Mexicans changed very decidedly after 1929 and repeatedly one hears politicians, miners and farmers who previously justified the contracting of Mexican labor at starvation wages denouncing the children or grandchildren of those immigrants and demanding that they be sent back to Mexico 'where they belong.' This is the idea generally held in these times; members of other nationalities are considered Americans after the second generation, but the Mexicans seem to be discriminated against and labelled with derogatory terms on all occasions. [7]

The attitude that prevailed during the depression years had its effect in the form of "repatriation" of the Mexicans to Mexico during the early 1930's. Thousands upon thousands were sent back to Mexico. Men were pulled from Works Progress Administration relief projects and loaded, families and all, on trains that carried them down into Mexico, where they were dumped on a land that was alien and hostile to their return. Katherine F. Lenroot, reporting on the social and economic repercussions of this action in the area of Nogales, Arizona, in 1943, stated:

> Children of repatriated Mexican parents, including many American-born children with alien parents, are causing great concern to the welfare authorities in these areas. It was reported that some 15,000 such children with their parents went through Nogales, Arizona, just across the border from Nogales, Mexico, on their way back to Mexico. Many of these children have drifted back to the United States, particularly older children, and are living from hand to mouth in Arizona. [8]

That the Mexican-Americans in Arizona had received ill-treatment in all respects because of the subservient economic standards to which they had been traditionally relegated was further evidenced by their markedly increased interest in eliminating those factors which had tended to keep them at such a level. There were several organizations, predominantly Mexican in membership, that were working to improve the conditions and inter-group relations of the Mexican-Americans in Arizona. This interest was not limited to the Mexicans alone. There were such organizations as the "Arizona Council for Civic Unity" and the labor union organizations, all diligently trying to improve the socio-economic status of the Mexican-Americans. The number of conferences and regional meetings on human relations and on the Spanish-speaking, as the people in areas other than Arizona preferred to be labeled, had increased considerably during the World War II and post-war periods. What the future holds for this group was best summarized by a comparison made between what Michael Scully[9] expressed regarding the Mexicans in Mexico and the attitude that prevailed in Arizona. Michael Scully observed:

> Many Mexicans have had a dislike and distrust of the United States, based largely on the natural human envy of heretofore impoverished people for the richest neighbor in the world. As machines and higher wages close the economic gap, and Mexicans become better fed, clothed and housed, that envy will give way to self-respect and neighborly cooperation.[10]

The general consensus of opinion that prevailed among the more successful Mexican-Americans of Arizona was that through greater recognition in the courts of justice, better educational opportunities, better teachers, and the opening of the doors of opportunity, the bitter experiences of the past would cease to be.[11]

VI. SUMMARY OF RELATED STUDIES

There was a definite lack of both published and unpublished material concerning the Mexican in Arizona. General studies that touched on Arizona gave only broad general conclusions. The available sources were primarily governmental pamphlets, bulletins, and reports of the various groups doing inter-group relations work in Arizona.

Other States. Texas, New Mexico, Colorado, and California, and four other states that were well represented in numbers of Mexican-Americans, had carried on extensive projects in determining the status of their Mexicans.

One of the most serious handicaps to the study of Spanish-speaking people in the southwest has been the lack of reliable population statistics. In order to carry out basic studies in this very important field of research, it is imperative that statistics on population and distribution, size of family, occupations, and socio-economic conditions be more fully developed. The Spanish-speaking people are not homogeneous group; they are not an easy one to delimit or define.[12]

Economic life should not depend on the misconceptions of a few. The notion that the Mexican is of an inferior race and that, as such, he is not entitled to wages on a par with his Anglo-American co-workers will be an obstacle in his upgrading.[13] The theory of race, as expounded by Count de Gobineau, had placed the Mexican in the group that was to be despised, ostracized, exploited and worked like a beast for starvation wages. The Mexican in Arizona has received much the same treatment as that accorded his forebears by the conquistadores and by the early captains of industry that made the Arizona soil produce by the sweat of the Mexican's brow.[14]

The magna charta of ideals that would give the Mexican, as well as the other minority groups, the freedom and equality which should have been theirs is to be found in the truly great national document of President Truman's Commission on Civil Rights. Itemized briefly these are the four essential American rights: (1) the right to safety and security of the person; (2) the right to citizenship and its privileges; (3) the right to freedom of conscience and expression; and (4) the right to equality of opportunity.

Some of the organizations that work toward the improvement of inter-group relations are the church-sponsored groups. Some are sponsored by communities, while others are sponsored by the educational institutions. In recent years Catholic, Jewish, and Protestant leaders have formed the National Conference of Christians and Jews. This group has financed such reports as that of the Greeley College Study in Intergroup Relations.[15]

Carey McWilliams, in his North from Mexico (1949), has presented an authoritative analysis and appraisal of the most dominant minority group in the Southwest. He discusses its northward migrations, its presence before the advent of the Anglo-American group, the number and the reasons why population statistics on the Mexican-Americans are mere approximations. Briefly he cites actual cases of discrimination. It is the most fundamental analysis of the Spanish-speaking in the Southwest.[16] His study, however, lacks specific information about his sources of reference.

Because of the growing interest in the development of better inter-group relations, there were many sources from which materials could have been gathered, but Arizona was, on the whole, the most poorly represented in the available bibliographies. The two better bibliographic sources were the Inter-American Occasional Papers, II,[17] and the Bibliographic Series No. 7.[18]

VII. ORGANIZATION OF THE STUDY

The material and data of this study were organized into three major areas of investigation as established by the terms of the problem stated.

Chapter I, the introductory chapter, was part of the first major area; it presented the statement of the problem, importance of the study, definition of terms used, scope of the study, methods of investigation, approach to the study, a historical delineation, and summary of related studies.

Chapter II, the second part of the first major area dealt with the immigration, motives for immigration, and population statistics.

Chapter III, the second major area, presented the economic aspects, discussed the factors creating the retarded economic status, and discussed the type of employment in which the Mexicans were to be found.

Chapter IV, the third major area and the last chapter on findings, presented and discussed the social aspects and institutions, i.e., the housing situation, the school, the home, and the church.

Chapter V, the final chapter, presented a summary which restated the findings and conclusions of the study.

FOOTNOTES

[1] Thomas Edwin Farish, History of Arizona (San Francisco: The Filmer Brothers Electrotype Company, 1916), III, 154.

[2] Ibid., p. 163.

[3] Carey McWilliams, North from Mexico (People of America Series, Philadelphia: J.B. Lippincott Company, 1949), p. 51.

[4] Cf. post, p. 20.

[5] McWilliams, op. cit., p. 129.

[6] Silvester Mowry, Arizona and Sonora (New York: Harper and Brothers Publisher, Franklin Square, 1864), p. 175.

[7] Rosalio Florian Munoz, "The Relation of Bilingualism to Verbal Intelligence and Social Adjustment among Mexican Children in the Salt River Valley, Arizona," (unpublished Master's thesis, Arizona State Teachers College, Tempe, Arizona, 1938), p. 4.

[8] Katherine F. Lenroot, "The Children's Bureau and Problems of the Spanish-Speaking Minority Groups," (unpublished mimeographed memorandum, United States Department of Labor, Children's Bureau, Washington, D.C., April, 1943), p. 1.

[9] Michael Scully, "New Life in Old Mexico," Reader's Digest, 48:45-48, February, 1946.

[10] Ibid., p. 48.

[11] Field notes: From interviews, Phoenix and Tucson areas. Jesus Franco, Carlos C. Morales, Jose R. Baca, Phoenix. Ernesto Munoz, Raul Castro, Genaro Manzo, et al., Tucson, June-July, 1950.

[12] Lyle Saunders, "The Spanish-Speaking Population of Texas," Inter-American Education, Occasional Papers V (Austin: The University of Texas Press, December, 1949), pp. 3-7.

[13] Most Reverend Robert E. Lucey, S.T.D., "The Spanish-Speaking of the Southwest and West," Social Action Department, National Catholic Welfare Conference (Report on the Conference of Leaders, July 20-23, 1943), pp. 24-25.

[14] Lombardo V. Toledano, "Judios y mexicanos o razas inferiores?" Universidad Obrera de Mexico (A Spanish language pamphlet, Mexico, 1942), pp. 1-34.

[15] Earl U. Rugg, "Intergroup Relations," Final Report 1946-1949, Greeley Committee, College Study on Intergroup Relations (Greeley, Colorado: Colorado State College of Education, April, 1949), pp. 1-19.

[16] Carey McWilliams, North from Mexico: The Spanish-Speaking People of the United States (Philadelphia: J.B. Lippincott Co., 1949), 324 pp.

[17]Clarice T. Whittenburg, and George I. Sanchez, "Materials Relating to the Education of the Spanish-speaking People," <u>Inter-American Occasional Papers II</u> (Austin: The University of Texas Press, February, 1948), 40 pp.

[18]Evelyn Apperson, "Mexican-Americans; A Selected Bibliography," <u>Bibliographic Series No. 7</u> (Chicago: American Council on Race Relations, mimeographed, 1949), 7 pp.

CHAPTER II

IMMIGRATION AND POPULATION

The original descendants of early Spanish or Mexican settlers, who were in the state prior to the Treaty of Guadalupe-Hidalgo and until the Territory of Arizona was given separate territorial status in 1863, represented approximately 12 per cent of those answering this investigator's questionnaire.[1] These people had been largely outnumbered by the immigration of Mexicans which began around 1910 and continued until 1930. Since the restrictions on crossing the border in either direction were almost unknown, the Mexican population of the state fluctuated constantly. In 1924, with the passage of the Immigration Act and the founding of the border patrol, immigration in unchecked numbers came to a halt. With such a background it was small wonder that the United States Census gave only approximations of their total numbers. The data presented in this study represented those figures cited by the United States Census for the period 1910-1948 and others as indicated.

I. MOTIVES FOR MIGRATIONS

The early colonists and Mexicans living in Arizona immediately following the founding of the missions were to be found working in the gold and silver mines of the "Apache-ridden" Sonora and Tucson area. After Mexico secured its independence from Spain in 1821,[2] the Mexicans continued to live in the southern portion of the state, so harassed by the Apaches that, by 1848, the Mexican population of Tucson had dwindled to a mere three hundred persons. With the advent of American troops and people in the 1860's, the number of Mexicans increased. The new industrial and agricultural enterprises needed laborers, and Sonora was the most ready source of supply. The Mexicans came in large numbers to fill the unskilled jobs created by the expanding mineral, agricultural, and railroad interests.

Immigration after 1900. Mexico was the second largest source of American immigration to the United States during the period 1901-1947. It contributed 788,000 recorded immigrants, 23 per cent of the total registered entries from the Western Hemisphere, and three fourths of all immigrants from Latin America.[3] The greatest period of immigration to the United States, from Mexico, occurred between 1900 and 1930. Railroad facilities in Mexico, as well as in the United States, had expanded to such an extent that transportation was available even for some of the poorest. Arizona's period of large immigration coincided with that of the rest of the nation, slackening off in the 1930 period. The Immigration and Naturalization Service[4] reported that in the 1900-1910 span, the number of immigrants went from 971 to 49,642. The next two decades saw this figure rise to 459,287 entrants from Mexico. There were many theories to explain why these people suddenly abandoned their villages and home ties, but the outstanding reason was an economic one. This investigator's survey indicated that, of those coming to Arizona, 76 per cent came for economic reasons; 8 per cent indicated their parents or antecedents came to Arizona because of the Mexican Revolution for Agrarian Reform of 1910; 8 per cent did not indicate a reason; and 8 per cent gave subjective reasons, such as "My father considered Mexico unfit for a half-breed to grow up in"; "To escape revolutionists who were causing much trouble at that time"; and others.[5] The survey questionnaire failed to indicate what percentage came as students or as professional men. That some had come as students or to practice their professions was learned from interviews with Mr. Raul Castro and Mr. Genaro Manzo of Tucson.[6]

It was thus evident that while the reasons for the great influx of Mexicans into Arizona were many, the economic reason stood out above the others. The fact had been further established that neighboring populations of low and limited economic resources were attracted to communities or nations having a higher standard of living and offering differentiated economic opportunities.

Religious persecution and political oppression played minor roles as motives for the immigration of Mexicans into Arizona. The Mexican Revolution of 1910 and after,[7] brought Mexican laborers into Texas and New Mexico to a greater extent. During this period of strife in Mexico, World War I broke out in Europe. Because

of the increased demand for American-made goods, and later because of the need
for labor to replace the men who left to serve in the American forces, Mexicans
were encouraged to come to fill the need for laborers. Many of the Mexicans in
Mexico, seeking to evade the ills at home, thought that by answering the call for
labor they would find a new life and new riches in the United States. They came
knowing well that here in the United States they would be faced with racial prejudice,
linguistic problems and cultural isolation. Those who came to Texas, New Mexico,
and California during that period had remained, for the large part, agricultural
workers. In discussing their plight and status, the report in Building America
stated:

> The Mexicans were welcomed as workers in the cotton fields of Texas,
> and on the truck farms of California where the irrigated vegetable and fruit
> crops required large numbers of field 'hands'. Letters from the few who
> came at first began to make their way back home. They told of a land free
> of revolutions, and of wages of $3 a day. Three dollars a day to a Mexican
> who was used to receiving the equivalent of fifty cents was 'like a million
> dollars'--a sum he could hardly understand. Then, agents of American
> employers began to cross into Mexico promising jobs to laborers, and
> even their travelling expenses.[8]

Although there was much useful information as to the motives behind the
coming of the Mexican to the United States, little data existed that contributed any
insight toward an understanding of the distribution, social problems and economic
trends of their native-born descendants that lived in Arizona. The majority of the
Mexicans that lived in Arizona were native-born, some had come from the neighboring states, some were of mixed national parentage, and a small percentage
were descendants of early prestatehood settlers.

II. POPULATION STATISTICS

The 1930 United States Census definition of the Mexican people as, "Those
born in Mexico or of Mexican parentage,"[9] was hardly the criterion for distinguishing
the group living in Arizona from the rest of the state's so-called Mexican population.
In Arizona there were many Mexican-Americans whose names were not of Spanish

origin, but who, otherwise, were culturally identified with the Mexican minority group. Bancroft, reporting on assimilation, stated, "Early emigrants to Arizona married easily into the Mexican population, it is not uncommon to find such names as Baker, Frank, Bateman, Thatcher, . . . "[10] Evidence of constant assimilation could be noted by the increasing number of marriages between the Anglo-American and the Spanish-name individuals of the Phoenix and Tucson areas.

Numbers. Gamio[11] reported that the Mexican population of Arizona according to the United States Censuses was 14,172 in 1900, and 61,580 in 1920. The 1930 Census figure indicated a total of 118,809, which represented approximately 23 per cent of the state's total population. The 1930 Census further gave indication that a high percentage of the Mexican population was native born, or second generation.

In an attempt to alleviate the injured pride of those who protested the 1930 census definition of the Mexicans, the 1940 census[12] tabulations did not list the Mexican separately but rather, if persons of Mexican birth or ancestry were not definitely Indian, or of other non-white race, they were returned as white. A special enumeration in 1942 based on that language spoken in the home of the person in his earliest childhood indicated that the state of Arizona had approximately 5.3 per cent of the total 1,864,000 white Spanish-mother-tongue persons in the United States,[13] a number ranging around 100,000 persons. This, then, indicated that during the depression period approximately 18,000 persons had left Arizona, for reasons of the depression or through repatriation. Arizona's total population figure for July 1, 1948, was 654,000 persons.[14] This figure represented an increase of 30.2 per cent over that of 1940. Assuming that Arizona's Mexican-American population grew in like manner, and that it represented 26 per cent of the state's total population, it would number around 130,000 persons. The 1950 tabulations from the United States Census had not yet been published at the time of this investigation.

Mexican Migratory Workers. During World War II the United States again experienced a shortage of labor in both the skilled and unskilled trades. Mexico, because of its proximity and its abundant number of agrarian people, was a ready source of supply. The influence these migrant workers, or Mexican Nationals, had on the total Arizona Mexican-American social and economic status was small since they were seasonal workers that came into the United States to work during the crop-harvesting seasons and returned to Mexico when the harvest was completed. Nevertheless, because of cultural ties and identification with the larger group, a survey of their conditions was conducted by this researcher.

Findings and trends indicated that since the end of World War II there was an increase in the number who entered as farm laborers. Some came from Mexico legally, but a large number entered illegally, a condition which trends indicate would continue for two important reasons: (1) as long as the economic conditions of Mexico remained in such a low position, legal as well as illegal entrants would continue to come into the United States in hope of finding profitable employment and (2) because of their docility and willingness to work for lower wages, alien laborers were encouraged by farmers and ranchers to enter legally or illegally. An article appearing in Border Patrol reports:

> These same farmers and ranchers state that . . . frankly . . . they prefer the illegal entrant to the American citizen laborer. They can pay him practically any wage they may desire, have to furnish him the very least of living facilities, and can in the majority of cases, control the movements of such aliens by threatening them with action by the Immigration Service.[15]

The number of illegal entrants varied from one thousand to five thousand yearly. During the three important cotton-picking months they were brought into Arizona by the Cotton Growers Association and Agricultural Commodities. These Mexican nationals were brought in to do agricultural work only in cases where they could not be filled locally by American workers. Regarding the whole situation, Mr. Ocelio Vasquez stated:

> Because the whole problem is more of an emergency program for securing of hands to harvest the crops, and because it is not a continuous one, the migrant workers and the Mexican nationals do not remain in the state as permanent population.[16]

These Mexican nationals were paid such low wages during the post-war period that often they returned to Mexico with a very small profit, if any, to show for their months of hard labor. Their economic plight, along with that of the Mexican-Americans, was given further consideration in the ensuing chapter.

The native-born Mexican-American population had increased in Arizona during the period 1940-50. Since immigration had largely been checked, the tendency was to rely on short-run, carefully controlled labor migration rather than permanent immigration.

FOOTNOTES

[1] Figure based on Questionnaire returns. Question 1, Part II. Questionnaire in Appendix.

[2] For a summarized analysis of Mexico during this period see Eileen Trimble Baker, "A Source Unit on the Republic of Mexico," (unpublished Master's thesis, Arizona State College at Tempe, Tempe, Arizona, 1948), pp. 57-58.

[3] Kingsley Davis, and Clarence Senior, "Immigration from the Western Hemisphere," Department of Justice Immigration and Naturalization Service, 7:31-39, September, 1949.

[4] Annual Report of the Immigration and Naturalization Service (Washington, D.C.: United States Department of Justice, Fiscal Year Ended June 30, 1948), n.p., Table 4.

[5] Figures based on computations from Questionnaire returns. Question 2, Part II, Family Inventory. Questionnaire in Appendix.

[6] Field notes: From interviews, Mr. Raul Castro and Mr. Genaro Manzo, Tucson, Arizona, June 27, 1950.

[7] For an extensive discussion on the Mexican Revolution see J. Alvarez del Vayo, The Last Optimist (New York: The Viking Press, 1950), p. 225.

[8] Society for Curriculum Study, Our Minority Groups: Spanish-Speaking People (Building America Series, Vol. 8, No. 5. New York: Americana Corporation), pp. 143-44.

[9] United States Bureau of the Census, Vol. III (1930 United States Census, Part I, Population), p. 1.

[10] Hubert Howe Bancroft, History of Arizona and New Mexico, 1530-1888 (The Works of Hubert Howe Bancroft. San Francisco: The History Company Publishers, 1889), XVII, p. 617.

[11] Manuel Gamio, Mexican Immigration to the United States: A Study of Human Migration and Adjustment (Chicago: University of Chicago Press, 1930), p. 24.

[12] United States Bureau of the Census, Vol. II, Characteristics of the Population, Part I (1940 United States Summary - United States Department of Commerce) p. 9.

[13] "New Census Returns and Education of our Spanish-Speaking Population," Education for Victory, 1:7-8, July 15, 1942.

[14] S. H. Steinberg, editor, "Arizona," The Statesman's Yearbook, 1949 (New York: The McMillan Company, 1949), p. 576.

[15] Helen F. Eckerson, and Nick D. Collaer, "Border Patrol," Department of Justice Immigration and Naturalization Service, 7:59, November, 1949.

[16] Field notes: Interview with Mr. Ocelio Vasquez, Agricultural Employment Assistant of the United States Employment Service, Phoenix, Arizona, June 20, 1950.

CHAPTER III

ECONOMIC ASPECTS

Arizona's Mexican-American population had carried the burden of undeserved poverty since early territorial days. Because of ignorance on their part and the lack of leadership material to guide them in united effort, they had been the object of ruthless exploitation by the big mining and agricultural industrialists. They had tasted the bitterness of low wages, poor housing, inadequate schools, job discrimination and public scorn for years. They were stereotyped as lazy, slow and improvident by their Anglo-American neighbors. Yet, these same neighbors never stooped to perform the essential menial tasks and hard physical labor for the same mere pittance offered the Mexican for his day's labor. The Most Reverend Robert E. Lucey addressed a group meeting to discuss the problems of the Spanish-speaking by posing these questions:

> How much exuberance, vitality and enthusiasm could any people show who had been underpaid, undernourished and badly housed for half a century? If the Mexican is sometimes illiterate, whose fault is it but the fault of those who denied him an education and drove him out to work in the days of his youth? If the Mexican is sometimes diseased and delinquent, whose fault is it but the fault of those who from his birth condemned him to poverty and squalor? If the Mexican is sometimes not a good American, what can you expect from a man who during all his life was socially ostracized, deprived of civil rights, politically debased and condemned to economic servitude?[1]

In this study, the economic factors underlying the retarded status of the Mexican people were taken into consideration. The argument was delimited primarily to a consideration of Arizona's Mexican people. In a study of this nature it was impossible to separate completely the economic aspects from the social aspects, therefore, this particular chapter included findings from both.

I. HISTORICAL ECONOMIC ASPECTS

Prior to and during territorial days in Arizona, the Mexican people were primarily gold and silver miners. The questionnaire survey used in this study gave indication that (1) Mexicans coming to Arizona prior to 1863 tabulated approximately 90 per cent as miners; (2) those coming in the period between 1863 and 1912 tabulated approximately 54 per cent in mining, 15 per cent in agricultural work, 29 per cent in diverse semi-skilled positions, and 1 per cent in skilled trades.[2] It was evident from the above breakdown that by 1912 the Mexican people were securing work in other than the mining industry. The types of positions were in the main of the semi-skilled type, i.e., construction work, cattle and stock care, adobe masons, railroad section hands, salesmen and small shopkeepers.

Traditionally the Mexicans in Arizona had received lower wages than the Anglo-Americans in the unskilled and in some of the semi-skilled trades. The tradition dated back to the early days of mineral expansion around the Sonora-Arizona border in the 1860's. Silvester Mowry said:

> The workmen at the furnace receive one dollar per day of twelve hours; Mexican laborers twelve to fifteen dollars per month, and to each man a ration of sixteen pounds of flour per week. American laborers are paid from thirty to seventy dollars per month and boarded . . . [3]

The practice of lower wages for the Mexican had carried through effectively until 1946. In that year the influence of organized labor, working toward improvement of the wages paid labor in Arizona, carried through some programs of investigation and court injunctions that had a large influence in remedying the situations in Arizona.

Job classification and wages. The wages paid the early day immigrants ranged from $1.25 a day to $3.25 a day in 1910. Wages increased from $4.00 to $6.00 per day for those coming to Arizona in the period, 1910 to 1920.[4] During the depression years from 1930 to 1940 wages were small or completely absent. The Mexican people of the state were well represented on the relief rolls. Mr. Roy Yanez, of Phoenix, stated, "At least 85 per cent of the Mexican people were still on relief in 1940."[5] Those not on relief during the depression years had salary ranges from \$1,000 to \$1,800 yearly.[6] The greatest change in wages and job classifications should have come during the World War II period but, actually, the change came in the post war period. In a summary of the situation in Arizona during 1944, Dr. Carlos E. Castaneda stated:

> . . . The mining industry of Arizona normally employs between 15,000 and 16,000 men. The percentage of Mexicans, that is American citizens of Mexican extraction in the main, is over 50% of the average and in many mining centers it runs as high as 80%. In round figures there are between 8,000 and 10,000 persons of Mexican extraction employed in the mining industry of Arizona. Their employment is restricted, however, very largely to common labor and semi-skilled jobs and even the urgent need of Manpower as the result of the war has not broken down the prejudice which bars large numbers of skilled laborers from promotion in order that they might be utilized at their highest skill and thus contribute more fully and more efficiently to the total war effort.[7]

The returning veterans and those persons who worked in war plants of the Pacific coast areas, having gained some understanding of life under better economic conditions, were eager to experience the same type of economic opportunities in Arizona. Their hopes were soon demolished. Those boys who had learned the intricacies of radar operation, flight control and flying itself were soon back in the pits and shafts of the mining camps or out picking lettuce and carrots in the agricultural areas. A small percentage were able to secure positions requiring technical skill; a fraction of 1 per cent of the returning veterans had found professional placement in the two larger cities of Tucson and Phoenix.[8] Generally the occupational opportunities had changed little, the areas of occupations were still limited, but organized labor was making itself felt.

II. AREAS OF OCCUPATIONS

The areas of occupations were distinct in Arizona. They were to be found in the rural mining towns in the agricultural districts, in the small farming communities where unskilled, semi-skilled and skilled labor predominated, and in the urban districts. The urban areas of occupations represented all the classifications of labor and professional types of employment.

Rural occupations. In the mining towns the primary occupations were those concerned with the production of copper. Those mining towns that had a sizeable number of Mexicans offered other opportunities to its Mexican-American populace in the form of small cafes, bars and saloons, clerking positions, recreational parlors and an occasional demand for skilled carpenters or masons.

The wages received by the Mexican miners were, as a result of strong union measures, far better than those of the early day miners. The traditional going rate of $1.00 a day had disappeared completely. The practice of paying the Mexican labor rate of $1.15 less per shift than that paid the Anglo-American helper ended in 1944 as a result of the injunction suits filed against the Miami Copper Company, the Inspiration Consolidated Copper Company and the International Smelter and Refining Company by the International Union of Mine, Mill and Smelter Workers, CIO, before the National War Labor Board on the charges that these three companies of Miami, Arizona, were practicing discrimination against non-Anglo employees.[9] Another incident of this nature was that which occurred in Ray, Arizona, involving the Kennecott Copper Corporation which had in the past practiced discrimination against its Mexican-American employees on a plan similar to that of the Miami group. In an arbitration case with the American Federation of Labor, which held contracts with it, the company lost because its contract was worded in such a manner that it discriminated against the Mexican-American employees. An article appearing in the Arizona Labor Journal of March 31, 1949, reported that the company was submitting a proposal to the American Federation of Labor for a change in the contracts. The article further reported that the ". . . company's representatives in that particular area do not like workers of Mexican birth and intend to see to it that they don't get a fair shake."[10]

Job discrimination was not a new thing in Arizona and was not limited to the mining companies alone. Evidence of these practices existed in the other fields where it had proved profitable to keep the Mexican at a lower wage, thus enabling the ranchers, farmers, store owners and company representatives to gain higher profits for themselves or their company through the exploitation of their employees.

Rural agricultural occupations. In Arizona most of the rural farmers or ranchers employed a small force of laborers for maintenance work or crop cultivation throughout the year. During the seasonal harvests they required a large supply of temporary labor for the harvesting of their crops. This labor force was almost wholly Mexican in number. Some of the people and their families remained on one farm throughout the year working either on the land itself or in the packing sheds, but the larger number was contract laborers who arrived under contract from Mexico or from the closest towns. A common sight in and around Phoenix during the different harvest seasons, was the early morning trucks packed with Mexican-American field hands departing to the fields or packing sheds. These field hands, recruited in the main from those having the lowest economic status, were abysmally poor. Their one and two room lumber shacks or their adobe huts could be seen lining the main irrigation canals leading into Phoenix, Scottsdale, Tempe, Litchfield, Buckeye and many other agricultural areas. Their earnings seldom exceeded $6.00 a day. The prevailing wage rate as of June, 1950, was sixty cents an hour for those working on a hourly basis. When interviewed concerning the reason these people continued to work at such low wages, Mr. Ocelio Vasquez stated:

> One reason they have hired out at such a low rate is that they find it to their advantage. By hiring out at a low rate they are able to use all hands in the family. During World War II many heads of families found that it was more profitable to stay in agriculture. By supplementing his wage with that of his family, a father and family often made from twelve to eighteen dollars a day. Had he sought employment in a war industry, he would have needed to resettle in some area where homes were hard to get, his would have been the only earnings, and unskilled labor among the Spanish-speaking has for the greater part remained unskilled and low paid.

> A noticeable trend since the end of the war has been that of the shift-over to urban industrial types of employment among the young men and veterans. These fellows are leaving the state to seek jobs that bring in a better income. They are scattering to industrial areas of the West coast and Midwest. [11]

The Mexican nationals who worked on a temporary basis as emergency "fieldhands," but whose acceptance had become an established policy, were often the subject of debate and discussion. Supposedly protected by inter-governmental agreements that guaranteed the worker payment at the prevailing wage rate, decent housing, compulsory accident insurance, free health examinations and medical services, elimination of deductions from wages for savings funds, and further guaranteed safe and adequate transportation, an eight-hour day, a maximum cost for meals and no work on Sunday; this group nevertheless lived in conditions no better than that of the native fieldhands. Mr. Ernesto Galarza of the National Farm Labor Union stated in a report, "Indeed, the August, 1949, Agreement extends to alien workers employed in the United States certain rights which domestic workers do not enjoy. The eight-hour day, free medical service and compulsory insurance provisions are examples of this inequality."[12]

However, the bright picture presented by such intergovernmental agreements had evidently not been successfully carried out. In June, 1950, President Harry S. Truman created a five-man commission to study the problem of illegal entries from Mexico and to study the conditions affecting the migratory workers of all kinds. An article appearing in the Arizona Daily Star on June 3, 1950, reported on this action by the President. The article reported:

> 'Previous studies have shown,' it said, 'that in many instances living standards among migratory workers and their families are markedly below those of other elements in the population, and that because of the absence of a fixed residence as well as their specific exemption in various laws, the migratory workers are frequently denied the benefits of federal, as well as state and local, social legislation.'[13]

This availability of cheap labor right across the Arizona border was an important factor in the development of Arizon's multi-million dollar agricultural industry. The Mexican nationals were used extensively in the Maricopa, Pinal, Pima and Yuma county farms and ranches. The men who made up the ranks of this type of manual workers came to the United States to do agricultural work regardless of the skill or trade they practiced in Mexico. The grower was required to do his own recruiting of labor and to furnish them with transportation to the United States and back to the place where they were hired in Mexico.[14]

Urban areas of occupation. The occupational opportunities open to the Mexican-Americans in the two larger cities of Arizona, Tucson and Phoenix, were far better than the opportunities in the rural areas. Tucson, because of its proximity to the Mexican border, surpassed Phoenix in the occupational opportunities offered the Mexican-Americans.

The greatest number of opportunities existed in the unskilled and semi-skilled positions of the construction field. Wages in these type of jobs ranged from $1.45 per hour in the semi-skilled categories to $2.02 an hour for the skilled worker. Non-union wages were far lower, depending entirely on the discretion of the employer.[15] Clerical help was amply represented in both cities. Employers in Tucson favored the hiring of Spanish-speaking individuals, regardless of national origin, for clerical and sales positions because of the huge number of Mexican-Americans in that city.[16] In Tucson, as in Phoenix, the Mountain States Telephone and Telegraph Company practiced a strict policy of non-employment of Mexican-Americans for clerical positions or as "operators." They based this company policy on the assumption that all Mexican-American girls have a language difficulty. Salesgirls, although hired in numbers proportionate to the population, were usually to be found in the "Bargain Basement" counters of the Phoenix department and novelty stores. The practice of placing their Mexican-American sales clerks in these specific spots was not strictly discriminatory. Much of the trade coming into Phoenix from the outlying agricultural areas was from the Mexican-American group, which sought out these bargain counters and thereby made Spanish-speaking clerks a practical asset to the store. Mrs. Placida G. Smith, a citizen of Phoenix since 1934, stated:

> When I first arrived in Phoenix the Mexican-American girls were hardly seen in any of the establishments around town. Now one sees them working in offices as secretaries, stenographers, beauticians, waitresses and sales clerks. Some of the girls have gone into the nursing profession and others are developing an interest in newspaper work. The young men have perhaps faced the greatest obstacles to securing permanent employment.

A few are doing leather-craft work, some are in the field of radio, some are working as sales clerks; still there is an obvious lack of vocational guidance for the Mexican-American youth still in school. Prior to World War II the majority of watchmakers and tailors were immigrant Mexicans or their sons. Today the Mexican-American boys are shying away from these highly skilled trades . . . [17]

The cooks and waitresses in the majority of the restaurants serving Mexican food in both Phoenix and Tucson, as well as in the mining towns, were Mexican-American girls. They represented approximately 26 per cent of the total membership in the organized hotel and restaurant employees' union. Their wages ranged from a minimum $4.00 a day for an eight-hour day to $11.00 for an eight-hour day. Higher wages were paid occasionally, but these, like those of non-union employees, were fixed at the discretion of the employer.

Mexican-Americans in the Teamsters' unions were poorly represented in number. Those members who did belong to unions earned wages ranging from $1.25 an hour to $2.02 an hour. Of the approximately two thousand members in the Teamsters' Union, American Federation of Labor, which represented the whole state, seventy-five Mexican-Americans were guaranteed work at salaries ranging from $29.87 to $54.55 per forty hour week. Ten Mexican-Americans who were driving trucks or making deliveries for the beer and liquor industries averaged $75.00 a week. Forty Mexican-Americans were driving for construction companies at wages ranging from $1.52 to $2.02 an hour.

In the packing house industry the majority of the common labor and skilled jobs were held by Mexican-Americans. Non-union packing houses paid wages ranging below the union scale which started at $1.04 an hour. Butchers of Mexican-American origin were seldom, if ever, hired in stores catering to Anglo-Americans. They were usually found working in areas where the Mexican people were a distinct group or where the Mexican-Americans constituted a large percentage of the neighborhood population.

Representation in the skilled trades was very poor in the Phoenix area and only slightly better in the Tucson area. Carpenters, both hourneymen and apprentices,

made up less than 10 per cent of the total number for the state. The Financial
Secretary at the Phoenix office of the Carpenters' and Joiners' Union stated:

> The low number of Mexican-Americans in the skilled trades is caused
> primarily by discriminatory practices on the part of the employers. Prior
> to 1935 there were no Mexican carpenters in the Phoenix union, although
> there were some around Tucson, Flagstaff and some of the mining towns.
> By 1940 we had a few in the Phoenix union and by 1950 a considerable num-
> ber were either in the union or trying to enter as apprentices. The Amer-
> ican Federation of Labor does not list the members separately under any
> nationality, therefore the 10 per cent mentioned is merely an approxima-
> tion.[18]

Carpenters' minimum wages began at $1.26 an hour for apprentices and at $2.10
an hour for journeymen.

Mexican-Americans seldom showed an interest in the electrical trades.
Representation in this area was definitely poor. Those young men who did take an
interest in the field left the state to secure employment. As in the carpenter trade,
the discriminatory practices of the employers had been the prime factor in turning
young men away from this high-paying trade.

The Mexican-Americans were better represented in the ironworkers and
steelworkers trades. The CIO affiliated union had a far larger number of semi-
skilled and skilled workers than the AFL affiliated union. The AFL representation
in the Phoenix area was very low, having only three Mexican-American members
out of two hundred listed members. Their wages ranged from $1.62 to $2.22 an
hour.[19]

One brotherhood of skilled tradesmen that would not permit Mexican-Americans to enter its ranks was the Railroad Brotherhood of Locomotive Engineers.
This statewide practice had always existed and apparently would continue for an
indefinite period of time.[20]

All evidence seemed to substantiate the fact that Mexican-Americans in the
urban areas of Arizona were still being kept out of the skilled crafts through the
discriminatory practices of Anglo-American employers and through the social pres-
sure applied by the buying public. In the mining towns there was a noticeable change

taking place through the efforts of the organized labor groups. In Clifton, Miami, Bisbee, and Superior, Mexican-Americans were being placed more and more in apprenticeship positions where their training and skill were the basis of selection.

The professional occupations. This area of occupations, covering both the urban and rural areas, indicated an overwhelming need for more Mexican-Americans in its ranks. The most evident need was in the field of education. Here, where the Mexican-American could undoubtedly do the most good for the group from which he stemmed, the lack of Spanish-speaking personnel was most noticeable. Of this tremendous lack of leadership material, Doctor George I. Sanchez has stated:

> . . . the Spanish-speaking people, in order to aid further in the solution of their problems, must develop to the fullest extent of their ability, and assume responsibility for their own development. More Spanish-speaking doctors, lawyers, social workers, teachers and members of the professions would aid in the promotion of individual and group welfare.[21]

The most unfortunate situation in Arizona, when leadership material had developed, was the not uncommon practice of the leaders' purposely losing their Mexican identity and letting their downtrodden fellowmen carry on as best they could. These leaders could not always be blamed completely for their acts. In Arizona, as in other sections of the Southwest and West, members of the Mexican-American group who were in the top social and economic level would be subject to social ostracism from their Anglo-American neighbors and business contacts if seen in the company of "those Mexicans." Victims of the competitive economic system which dictates their living patterns, these Mexican-Americans, usually relabeled "Spanish", could not be held entirely to blame for the loss of their sense of social responsibility.

Professional opportunities were limited in all areas of Arizona. Tucson, Nogales, Yuma and Phoenix were the only areas indicating the presence of any professional men, other than teachers,[22] and these in a very small number. Tucson had had professional men from among its Mexican-American citizenry since the early years of statehood, while in Phoenix and the other towns they had been represented only since 1940. Arizona's Mexican-American professional people represented less than 0.1 per cent of the total number of professional individuals.[23] In an effort to determine the reason for such a small percentage, this investigator asked the following question of all those interviewed: "What could be the reason for such a poor showing in this area of occupations?" The general consensus of opinions was that the poor showing was due to (1) the lack of financial means on the part of the individuals who wanted to enter the professional fields; (2) the existent low economic status of the Mexican-Americans generally; (3) the disillusionment caused by job discrimination; (4) the restriction in the establishment of a practice to Tucson or Phoenix where the established competition was such that they were forced to accept mediocre positions or to leave the state in search of better conditions; and (5) the evident need of better vocational guidance for the youth of Mexican-American descent. The consensus of opinion regarding the outlook for the future was that through the improvement of educational facilities, greater assimilation and improved cooperation between the Anglo-Americans and the Mexican-Americans a change in the whole area of occupations could be expected. The number of Mexican-Americans who owned and operated their own businesses had steadily increased throughout the years. Some had amassed considerable holdings in the grocery, dry goods, furniture and recreational industries, as well as in the various other forms of financial enterprises.

Other areas of occupations. A person visiting any one of the towns in Arizona wherein the Mexican-American people had their own community or lived in distinct areas would have encountered the small shops, cafes, bars, beauty shops and grocery stores operated by their respective owners. The pride of ownership and independent business, regardless of mediocre financial success, was still a strong culturally inherited trait among these particular Mexican-Americans. Had the person passed through the same town twenty or thirty years earlier, he would have seen the strong influence of the Mexican folk culture vividly at work. Here were a people who, transplanted to the American scene, were doing exactly as they and their parents had previously done in Mexico. There were the early morning menudo, tamale and pan-dulce sellers,[24] noisily peddling their wares; then, as the activity of the day increased, the varied sellers of wares, lugging their merchandise with them from door to door, carried newspapers, insurance, clothes, legal advice and fresh staples to their customers. In the evenings the raspada vendor would push his cart around, stopping to sell his crushed ice delicacy to the young men and women out for the evening's promenade.

The acquisition of the American business methods and economic concepts began to change the picture in the Mexican colonies. Small stores, newsstands and small offices had replaced the door to door sellers by 1940. By 1950 the practices of the past had largely disappeared. Occasionally, in the predominantly Mexican-American areas, one would see the menudo vendor or insurance man doing business from door to door, but now he no longer travelled on foot: his mode of transportation was the automobile. The little stores had grown larger, some having even moved into town. The insurance peddlers and scribes now had offices in town, while the other assorted enterprisers had blossomed forth as proprietors of furniture stores, drugstores, jewelry shops and countless other small businesses. A series of articles appearing in the Spanish-language newspaper Voces (1949)[25] gave an account of how the Mexican-Americans in the Phoenix area were succeeding in their commercial pursuits and in their social relations among themselves and with the Anglo-American group.

The earnings of this group were mere estimates. No exact figures could be gathered since the majority of those interviewed, or of those who returned the survey questionnaire, were reluctant to divulge this information. The returns indicated a bottom yearly income of $1,200 and the highest returns indicated a yearly income of $8,000. The cluster came at the $3,000 level.[26]

Civil Service employees from the Mexican-American group constituted approximately 30 per cent of the postal employees in the Phoenix and Tucson areas.[27] Civil Service representation in the state and city offices, however, was better in the Tucson area.

Although the Mexican immigrant was predominantly a low paid manual worker, his children and grandchildren had branches out into other occupations and fields of endeavor. His economic position had improved, but only slightly. The door of economic opportunity and social acceptance was still, on the whole, closed to the greater number of Mexican-Americans.

FOOTNOTES

[1] Most Reverend Robert E. Lucey, S. T. D., "Are We Good Neighbors?" The Spanish Speaking of the Southwest and West (Washington, D.C.: Social Action Department, National Catholic Welfare Conference, 1943), p. 14.

[2] Figures based on Questionnaire returns. Question 1 and 10, Part II, Family Inventory. Questionnaire in Appendix.

[3] Silvester Mowry, Arizona and Sonora (New York: Harper and Brothers Publisher, Franklin Square, 1864), p. 166.

[4] Figures compiled from Questionnaire returns. Question 10, Part II. Questionnaire in Appendix.

[5] Field notes: Interview with Mr. Roy Yanez, Assistant Director of the Phoenix Housing Authority, Marcos de Niza Project, Phoenix, Arizona, June 22, 1950.

[6] Figures averaged from Questionnaire returns. Questions 6, 7, and 8, Part I. Questionnaire in Appendix. (Salaries represented are those of store owners, public utilities workers, and others not agricultural workers, or miners.)

[7] Carlos E. Castaneda, "Statement before the Senate Committee on Labor and Education in the Hearings held September 8, 1944, on Senate Bill 2048" (Special Assistant to the President's Committee on Fair Employment Practice. Mimeographed. Washington, D.C.), p. 2.

[8] Cf. post, p. 75.

[9] Carey McWilliams, North from Mexico, op. cit., pp. 196-99.

[10] News item in the Arizona Labor Journal, American Federation of Labor publication, March, 1949.

[11] Field notes: Interview with Mr. Ocelio Vasquez, Agricultural Employment Assistant of the United States Employment Service. Phoenix, Arizona, June 20, 1950.

[12] Ernesto Galarza, Mexican-United States Labor Relations and Problems, Summarized Proceedings III (mimeographed, Albuquerque: Fourth Regional Conference, Southwest Council on Education of the Spanish-Speaking People, Jan.23-25, 1950), p. 1.

[13] News item in the *Arizona Daily Star* (Tucson, Arizona), June 5, 1950.

[14] Field notes: Public Law 45, United States Department of Agriculture, 1917. Source: Interview with Mr. Ocelio Vasquez, June 20, 1950.

[15] Field notes: Interview with Secretary of the Construction Production and Maintenance Laborers Union, Local No. 383. Phoenix, Arizona, June 22, 1950.

[16] Field notes: Interview with Mrs. R. Gallegos, Alianza-Hispano-Americana Fraternal Service Director, Tucson, Arizona, June 27, 1950.

[17] Field notes: Interview with Mrs. Placida G. Smith, director of the Friendly House, 802 S. First Avenue, Phoenix, Arizona, June 28, 1950.

[18] Field notes: Interview with the financial secretary of the American Federation of Labor Carpenter's and Joiner's Union, District Council of Carpenters, Phoenix, Arizona, June 22, 1950.

[19] Field notes: Interview with Mr. Joe R. Baca, President of the United Steelworkers of America, CIO, Phoenix, Arizona, June 22, 1950.

[20] Field notes: Interview with Mrs. Placida G. Smith, Director of the Friendly House, Phoenix, Arizona, June 28, 1950.

[21] George I. Sanchez, editor, *First Regional Conference on the Education of the Spanish-speaking People in the Southwest* (The Inter-American Education Occasional Papers I. Austin: University of Texas Press, 1946), p. 13.

[22] The placement opportunities and limitations for Mexican-Americans in the field of education are discussed further in Chapter IV, p. 74, of this study.

[23] Field notes: Percentage number computed from data furnished by Mrs. Placida G. Smith, Phoenix, Mr. Ernesto Munoz, and Mr. Raul Castro, Tucson, and researcher's survey, June, 1950.

[24] *Menudo.* A spicy, hominy dish. Prepared with calf's stomach, corn, onions and assorted spices. *Tamale.* Cooked corn with either a chili-meat or sweetened center, wrapped in corn husks and cooked. *Pan-dulce.* Sweet breads. Usually served with coffee or chocolate. A favorite for afternoon snacks.

[25] Editorial series appearing in *Voces, La Revista del Noroeste* (Ciudad Obregon, Sonora: Enrique Robles Medina, editor-owner), Vol. V, Nums. 40-47, April-August, 1949.

[26] Figures based on reported salaries. Question 5, Part I of Questionnaire. Salaries indicated as of June 17, 1950. Questionnaire in Appendix.

[27] Percentage based on Spanish-name selection. Post Office Department Files, Phoenix, Arizona, June 15, 1950.

CHAPTER IV

SOCIAL ASPECTS

The retarded economic, educational, cultural and community social status of the Mexican in Arizona had been the underlying cause for much discussion and controversy prior to the time of this investigation. In this study a survey of their housing conditions, educational opportunities and the social institutions was undertaken in an attempt to present the facts as they had been and were at the time of the survey.

I. HOUSING

General conditions. When John Gunther stated, "The cleanest city I saw in America was Phoenix, Arizona,"[1] he made an erroneous conclusion, or perhaps he failed to visit the section of the city lying immediately south of the Southern Pacific Railway tracks. The Phoenix slum section presented conditions that could easily be duplicated in almost any other town or village in Arizona. During the period of great immigration, 1910 to 1930, the most common sight in the rapidly expanding mining and farming towns of Arizona was that of the unpainted lumber shacks and the outdoor privy. Mexican-town was easily spotted in those early days, and by 1950 conditions had improved only slightly.

Housing, Phoenix area. Although Phoenix had gained a world wide reputation for its cleanliness, health regaining facilities and beautiful homes, the existing housing conditions had never been as good as they might have been. Efforts on the part of such organizations as the Arizona Council for Civic Unity, the labor organizations, church organizations and civic groups had done much toward improving the slum areas of Phoenix. The first housing improvement came in 1941, as the direct result of the efforts of a former Catholic priest, Emmett McLaughlin,[2] and some civic minded individuals who assisted him in obtaining Federal and state funds.

The problem which gave rise to the improvement program of Emmett McLaughlin was a familiar one. Families in the lowest income group could not afford either to buy or to rent good standard housing, they were obliged to live in blighted areas where the rents were low.

In 1937 Federal aid to communities having areas with substandard housing was made available through the U.S. Housing Act, but Phoenix did not profit by the Act until 1941. In an interview with Mr. Roy Yanez, the following data concerning low rent housing in Phoenix were obtained. He stated:

> . . .'Father Emmett' as he was then known, persuaded the Arizona Legislature to adopt housing legislation. Then through his efforts and those of other interested individuals the city of Phoenix established in 1941 the office known as the Housing Authority of the City of Phoenix. This office then allotted funds for conducting a survey to determine the slum conditions of Phoenix. Once determined, Federal aid was granted and work was begun on three separate projects. These three went into operation, on a non-profit basis, in June, 1941.[3]

The original intention was to construct three separate units: Matthew Henson for Negroes, Marcos de Niza for Mexican-Americans, and Frank Luke, Jr. for the Anglo-American group. During World War II, and immediately thereafter, two other units were opened for the returning veterans. Although not of permanent-type construction as the original three, they had functioned properly up to the time of this study.

The Matthew Henson, Marcos de Niza and Frank Luke, Jr. projects were of masonry construction. They had a bathroom, one or two bedrooms, a living room and a kitchen with all facilities included. Families with two or less minor dependents were charged one fifth of their yearly income as rent. If the income exceeded $2,040, the tenants were asked to leave. Families with three or more minor dependents were permitted to remain only if their maximum yearly salary did not exceed $2,430. Rents charged ranged from $10 a month to $34 a month, the average being $26 a month, utilities included. There were between 2,500 and 3,000 persons living in the 604 units of the three projects.[4]

Conditions in the Phoenix slums were still deplorable in June, 1950. The conditions were to be improved somewhat through the addition of five hundred new units. An article in the Arizona Republic of June 18, 1950, reported:

> . . . The housing authority plans to build the new developments near existing projects: 144 units immediately south of the present Marcos de Niza Homes . . . 218 units immediately west of Matthew Henson Homes . . . and 138 units near Frank Luke, Jr. Homes . . .

Although this project was not technically a part of the Public Housing Administration's slum clearance program, many of the substandard dwellings in the Metropolitan Phoenix Area were thus to be eliminated.[5]

Housing, Tucson area. The Tucson area presented a housing condition similar to the Phoenix area. While lumber shacks predominated in the Phoenix slum districts, adobe huts were more prevalent in the Tucson districts, with a scattering of lumber shacks in the southern part of the city. Unlike Phoenix the Tucson housing problem had not been one of the social discriminatory type, but rather one of economics. Since a large percentage of the population had always been Mexican-Americans and since they had always lived in areas of their own choice, there were no true restrictive residential areas which tended to keep them out through discriminatory measures. Those Mexican-Americans who had lived in distinctive areas prior to the rapid growth of the city during World War II had tended to remain in those areas. No problem existed for those who desired to move into other residential areas. If they had the financial resources and were able to secure the land in a neighborhood of higher socio-economic standing, there was little or no social resistance present.

Low rent housing for those of the lower income groups unable to afford standard housing was negligible. One small housing project existed but was inadequate for the needs of the people. The issue of low rent housing for the lower income groups was under consideration at the time this survey was conducted in June, 1950. Tucson, like Phoenix, was attempting to secure governmental aid through the Federal Housing Act of 1949. The voters in Tucson were to vote on September 26, 1950, on two propositions that would secure five hundred public housing units for all groups.[6]

Housing, other areas of Arizona. Perched precariously on a hillside over-
looking Miami, Arizona, were to be seen the lumber shacks of the Mexican-Americans, while across the small valley on the opposite hillside were to be seen the
houses of the Anglo-Americans. Lining the Miami Wash, at the west end of the
town, were two continuous rows of dilapidated Mexican shacks; that was Miami until
1948. In that year the Miami Townsite Office, owners of the tracts on which these
miserable hovels were located, adopted a policy for eliminating these eyesores.
Presenting a dictum to the Mexican-Americans of either "move out or sell out, "
the people had no alternative but to move. Thus came moving-day for many of the
Mexican-Americans. The shacks were moved, at an exorbitant cost to the families,
to areas where passing tourists would not be faced with the eyesore these shacks
had created. The newly cleared areas were zoned and declared "restricted, " and
the complaints of the Mexicans went unheeded. The scenes presented by the Mexican canyons (the name applied to streets where Mexican-American families predominated in number), in and around Miami were characteristic of the scenes presented by any Mexican-town in Arizona. Evident always were the lumber shacks
leaning to right or to left or half submerged in debris left by summer storms; the
ever present small grocery store; the pool hall; the lack of street lights; the rudi-
mentary sanitation facilities; and the police protection only when "total war" took
place. Characteristic also were the scenes over the hill in the next canyon. Here
in the exclusively Anglo-American district were the paved streets, the good lighting,
the regular garbage collection service, and the highly prized inside toilet facilities.

The study conducted by this investigator indicated that the type of house construction predominating in the areas in which those answering the questionnaire
lived were (a) wood frame, 60 per cent, (b) brick or concrete block, 20 per cent,
(c) stucco frame, 10 per cent, (d) adobe block, 8 per cent, and (e) concrete construction, 2 per cent.[7] The study further revealed that 52 per cent lived in a mixed
community of Anglos and Mexicans and 48 per cent lived in a distinctive area; 4
per cent of the latter group indicated that only a few Mexican-American families
were allowed in the exclusive Anglo-American residential districts of their

community.[8] In a similar survey conducted in 1947 by Doctor Roy C. Rice of Arizona State College at Tempe, he reported that in 68.5 per cent of the farming areas and small towns the people mixed and mingled as they pleased. In the remaining 31.5 per cent, the people lived in distinct areas with the Mexican group being the most distinctive group represented.[9] Doctor Rice's study was based on a questionnaire sent to Arizona secondary school principals and administrators.

In an effort to establish the up-to-dateness of the kitchen facilities present in Mexican-American houses, the question, "Do you own a refrigerator? Electric or gas range?" was included in the questionnaire. The responses indicated that 92 per cent owned refrigerators, 60 per cent owned gas ranges, 24 per cent were still using wood-burning ranges and 16 per cent did not indicate which type of range they owned.[10]

A comparison to indicate the relative condition of the bathroom facilities of the mining towns and those of the rural agricultural areas indicated that 80 per cent of the houses in mining towns had indoor toilet and bath facilities, while only 10 per cent of the rural houses had both facilities present. A further analysis of the mining towns indicated that houses belonging to the mining company were almost all equipped with both the facilities.[11]

The fact was thus established that the housing conditions in all areas of Arizona needed improvement. The low rent areas were virtually slum districts. Phoenix had inaugurated a housing program in 1941 that was still expanding in 1950. Tucson had yet to start a housing program to reduce the number of substandard dwellings for its low income groups. A noticeable trend was the increasing modernity of kitchen equipment; a high per centage had refrigerators in their homes. Bathroom facilities, on the other hand, were not as available nor as modern as refrigerators.

II. THE SCHOOL

The fundamental principles of education and of human decency had suffered immeasureable abuse in the state of Arizona. The practices of the past had not been entirely in keeping with the concept that the school was a social institution which helped the young acquire the predominating culture of the community. Segregation of the Negro in Arizona, sanctioned by state laws,[12] had been extended in many localities to include the Mexican-American children. The excuses given by those upholding these acts of discrimination had bordered on the fantastic. The more common excuses given were (1) that the children were separated on the basis of language difficulty and (2) that the mixing of the Anglo-American and the Mexican-American children had tended to retard and impede the education of the former.

The fault for the continuation of these practices had not been entirely in the school itself, for the Mexican-American parents had too often failed their children through their inability to organize and combat legally these malpractices permitted by the elected school officials.

Discrimination had extended even further in the state's educational policies; Mexican-American college and University graduates had encountered it in almost all the professional fields they tried to enter. Opportunities were so limited for this group that often they left the state to secure professional placement.

Education of the early Mexicans. The first interest in the education of the Mexicans in Arizona dated back to pre-territorial days in the missions of southern Arizona. The Catholic church had a mission school at San Xavier del Bac, near present day Tucson, which served both the Mexican and the Papago children. In his History of Arizona, Farish stated:

> . . . at the mission of San Xavier del Bac, Padre Messaya has, at great trouble and expense to himself educated all children free of charge. His pupils are Mexican and Papago; he has been sadly impeded in his efforts by want of suitable school books.[13]

This was the first school opened in the area now known as the state of Arizona. In 1868 a school exclusively for boys was founded in Tucson. Jennie Ellingson, writing in 1910, stated, ". . . there was founded in Tucons a school for boys. Here, with perhaps a half a dozen books in a small adobe house, Augustus Brichta taught for six months fifty-five Mexican boys."[14]

Facilities in these early schools were very limited. The evident need was taken into consideration by a group in the state's Legislature and funds were appropriated later for the mission school and the Tucson school.

Educational segregation. School secregation had been the central topic of many discussions and conferences in Arizona, but until 1950 very little action had taken place to eliminate it. The Mexican people of Miami, Glendale, Tolleson, Douglas, Safford, Duncan, Tempe, and many other towns had all experienced the effect of discriminatory practices in the schools of the community. They had seen their children grow, attend the public schools, complete their schooling and still speak English with the Mexican accent so commonly popularized by the ignoble radio comedians in their efforts to produce laughter. These same Mexican people had too often remained docile when they could have helped remove this situation by organizing or putting into office the people who were sympathetic to their plight. In 1950 the prevailing attitude among the various organizations interested in eliminating the practice of school segregation was one of opposition to all forms of racial discrimination.[15]

On June 6, 1950, Ralph Estrada and Greg Garcia, Phoenix attorneys, and A.F. Wirin, a Los Angeles attorney, filed in the United States District Court at Phoenix a preliminary injunction suit[16] asking the court to compel the school board and officials of Tolleson School District No. 17 to admit to pupils of Mexican descent the use of facilities provided for the children of Anglo-American descent in Unit 1 school on the south side. The school in use by the Mexican-American students at the time had few facilities or provisions for the children's comfort and enjoyment. It was felt by the Mexican-American parents being represented that the action of the school board was such that the health, rights and privileges of the students of Mexican descent were being infringed upon.

This action by a citizens' committee in the interest of better education represented a heretofore unprecedented act on the part of the Mexican people. The stand taken by the school officials, i.e., Ross L. Scheely, James W. Johnston, Frank E. Babcock[17] and Kenneth Dyer, Superintendent, was that the segregation that was practiced was not discriminatory. The reason given for the practice was that of the language-difference problem, which had been the reason offered in

-40-

previous injunction suits in other states.

A news item appearing in the Arizona Republic reported on a similar case filed in Orange County, California. The presiding judge, Paul J. McCormick expressed this judgment:

> The evidence clearly shows that Spanish-speaking children are retarded in learning English by lack of exposure to its use because of segregation . . . . Co-mingling of the entire student body instills and develops a common cultural attitude which is imperative for the perpetuation of American institutions and ideals. Segregation fosters antagonism in the children . . . and suggests inferiority where none exists.[18]

Doctor George I. Sanchez of the University of Texas had written, concerning the continued practice of separate instruction for children from the Spanish-speaking group, that:

> In any case, separate instruction because of language reasons cannot be justified, except in rare instances for individuals, beyond the first year of school attendance of any child. If there were continued need for such separate instruction, that in itself would be evidence that the separate instruction was inadequate and uncalled for and, therefore, discriminatory . . . . In the last analysis, separate classrooms for language groups, such as the Spanish-speaking group, have been Civil, District Court of the United States, Western District of Texas: Minerva Delgado, et al vs. Bastrop Independent School District of Bastrop County, et al, June 15, 1948: and the Mendez case, Ninth U.S. Circuit Court of Appeals, April 14, 1947) . . . .[19]

In June, 1950, a petition was being circulated in Arizona by the organized labor groups and by the Arizona Legislative League for the purpose of placing on the November ballot an initiative measure which would amend the statutes which then permitted school trustees to practice segregation in the public schools of Arizona. The new act was to enfore the proposed ruling that segregation would no longer be permitted " . . . for reasons of race, creed, color or national origin, nor shall any distinction be made on account of race, creed, color or national origin."[20] The choice of repealing the segregation laws of the state was, therefore, being left to the citizens of the state.

The Segregation pattern. In a study presented in 1949 by the Arizona Council for Civic Unity it was pointed out that segregation practices in the state of Arizona followed no definite established pattern. The study reported that ". . . there is no such thing as an 'Arizona pattern.' Segregation (not only for Negroes, but also of Indian and Spanish-speaking students) varies from community to community--. . ."[21] The report further mentioned that the following towns still had segregated schools, or practiced segregation of the Mexicans in some form: Ajo, Douglas, Flagstaff, Glendale, Tolleson, Safford and Duncan.[22] The survey conducted by this investigator turned up a few more, i.e., Miami, Superior and Clifton.[23] Attempting to determine the Mexican-American parents' reaction to the practice of segregation, Question 9 of the questionnaire asked them to give a short statement expressing the reason school administrators in their community gave for the continued practice of segregation. All returns indicated that the language-difficulty and the ensuing retardation of the Anglo-American child were the predominant reason given.[24] An interview with a former Miamian who attended the public schools of that district presented a different answer. She attributed their practice to the fact that "many of the early administrators were of Texas sympathy or origin, thus, they discriminated against the Mexicans on the general basis that Mexicans were just Mexicans and as such were to be treated accordingly." She continued, "after 1928 the administrators have given just whatever reason they wished to give."[25]

Some of the school districts in Arizona were almost totally Mexican-American. In districts of this type the predominance of Mexican-Americans was such that the school's student population was made up entirely from children of this group. Tucson, which had been one of the more favorable cities for intergroup relations, had in the past permitted the Anglo-American children to transfer from the school in their district to another school if they desired to attend a school with less Mexican-American children. A report of the proceedings of the Tucson Council for Civic Unity discussed and clarified the segregation practices of that area thus:

. . . with redistricting and the construction of new schools, this practice will end, and they will have to attend school in the district in which they live. The new policy will lead to more integration than has been the case in the past.[26]

Other communities in Arizona practiced segregation regardless of what district the children lived in or whether or not they were proficient in English. One district openly transported the Mexican-American children across town to the "Mexican-school," then transported the Anglo-American children, who lived close to this school, past the school on the way to the "Gringo's school."[27]

Teachers and employment opportunities. If Spanish-name selection was any criterion for determining the types of opportunities that were open to the Mexican-Americans in the schools of Arizona, then they were categorically limited almost wholly to the unskilled and semi-skilled positions of custodians, janitors, cafeteria help and occasionally of secretaries. Data based on figures compiled from the Arizona Educational Directory for the school year 1949-1950 indicated that of the 4,777 elementary and high school teachers in the state, approximately 1.5 per cent were Spanish-name or known to be Mexican-Americans.[28] The reasons behind such poor representation of Mexican-Americans in this professional area were many. In his investigation of intergroup relations as they existed in Arizona's secondary schools, Doctor Roy C. Rice found that:

> . . . In Arizona there are definite objections to the hiring of members of the minority groups . . . . Fifteen per cent of the schools object to the hiring of Spanish-Americans (or Mexicans) as Spanish teachers, while 21 per cent of the schools object to members of this group teaching in other areas of instruction.[29]

A further analysis of the Arizona Educational Directory for the 1949-1950 school year indicated that there were 20 Spanish-name teachers instructing in fourteen of the state's seventy high schools. Of the number listed, 8 were teaching in areas other than Spanish. Of the 3,582 elementary school teachers, 52 were Spanish-name. A comparison analysis for the first year of each decennial period preceding the 1949-1950 period indicated that less than 1 per cent of the teachers listed in the Arizona Educational Directory for the 1939-1940, 1929-1930 and for the 1914-1915 school years were Spanish-name. In the 1914-1915 Directory there were only 4 elementary school teachers listed from a combined high school and elementary school total of 1,150 teachers.[30]

Spanish-name elementary school board members had always had better representation than Spanish-name teachers. In 1914-1915 there was a total of 406 board members of which twenty were Spanish-name. In 1929-1930 there were approximately 1,106 elementary school board members of which fifty-five were Spanish-name. In 1940-1941 there were approximately 955 elementary school board members of which thirty-seven were Spanish name. High school board members have always had less than 1 per cent representation, if any. The 1949-1950 comparison indicated that there were forty-one Spanish-name elementary school board members in the 256 elementary school districts and two Spanish-name high school board members in the 62 high school districts.

Since the end of World War II there had been a noticeable increase in the number of Mexican-Americans attending the state's institutions of higher learning. Mr. Ernesto Munoz of Tucson commenting on this increase stated:

> The Mexican-American young man of today is showing a greater interest in securing a better education. They are surging ahead despite the obstacles and lack of opportunities for professional placement. This is in evidence around the University, here in Tucson. The Mexican boys are active participants in the various colleges on the campus. This year Valdemar Cordova, a Phoenix student, was student body president of the Law School. Others have been active in campus affairs and in some of the fraternities. Still, many of these fellows have had to leave the state after completing their studies: opportunities are still too limited here. Those that do obtain good positions serve to inspire other Mexican-Americans into coming to school.[31]

This trend and the fact that the Mexican-American parents had finally organized in one section of the state to combat injustice and discrimination, indicated that although the social pressures of the past have often seemed unsurmountable, they have nevertheless made a scant showing in the roles of teacher and pupil.

There was also an indication that opportunities for this group needed to be increased if they were to aid in the promotion of their individual and group welfare.

III. THE HOME

The Mexican-American home presented those factors which had served to identify them most specifically as a distinct separate cultural group from the rest of the Americans in Arizona. Although some change had taken place throughout the period of slow acculturation, nevertheless, some traditions and cultural traits had resisted the strong influence of American customs and traits.

Changes in home life. Home life for the early Mexican settlers and immigrants into Arizona was not too far different from that life which they had previously lived in Mexico. Religious objects were always in evidence around the home, the language spoken was always Spanish, food was distinctly Mexican in style of preparation and flavor and family recreation consisted in spending long hours in friendly conversation or in listening to Mexican music. The great influx of Anglo-Americans and their cultural patterns began to make a few changes in the home life of the Mexicans. The younger members of the family soon acquired the language, tastes and mannerisms of the Anglo-Americans. Religion became a secondary thing; where previously the family had attended evening services as a group, they now went separate ways. The young men and women sought out the places of recreation along the "main streets," the parents continued in the established patterns of their fathers. This clash of cultures was still in strong evidence at the time this study was carried out.

It has been stated that the Mexican group has been one of the most difficult to assimilate or Americanize. In this study the writer attempted to discover what some of the factors causing this retardation were. Because language was perhaps the strongest factor, a question in the survey questionnaire asked, "Did your parents speak English?" The returns indicated that of the fifty responses to this question, 60 per cent had parents that did not speak it. The responses to the question, "Do you speak Spanish at home? English? Both?" indicated that 16 per cent speak only Spanish, 0 per cent spoke only English, and 84 per cent spoke both languages.[32]

Spanish-language newspapers, along with the radio, had been strong factors in the retarded Americanization of the group. Spanish-language newspapers had always been available to the Mexican-Americans in Tucson since 1877, and to the Mexican-Americans in Phoenix since 1883. The first of its kind was probably the Dos Republicas of Tucson. Three other Spanish-language newspapers of that same period were the Tucson Fronterizo of 1878, C. J. Velazco, editor, the Phoenix Union of 1883, Aguirre and Celis, editors, and the Mercurio of 1884, F. T. Davila, editor.[333]

In an interview with Mrs. Josefina C. Franco, editor of the El Sol, she presented these data:

> In 1903 there was in Phoenix a small weekly known as El Mensajero, whose editor was a Senor Mendez. Tucson had in 1915 El Tucsonense which was the property of Rosa Moreno. Its publisher was Arturo E. Moreno, and lately its editor was Ricardo Fierro. The El Sol, of which I am the present editor, was first known as Justicia, under Pedro de la Lama in 1922, and became known as El Sol in that same year. Today it is a weekly newspaper whose policy is one of presenting general news of interest to all, but especially for the improvement of the Mexican people and their intergroup relations. We strive to put down the practices of discrimination and aid in charities affecting all groups.[34]

There were other Spanish-language newspapers entering the homes of the Mexican-American people in 1950. Some were from Los Angeles, California, or from El Paso, Texas. Spanish-language magazines were sold in Phoenix and Tucson, but the rest of the state received very little material of this nature. No mention was made in this study of the sporadix Spanish-language newspapers that had, on the basis of political or specific issues, appeared briefly in the various mining towns of the state.[35]

One of the primary factors hindering the complete acculturation (or Americanization) of the Mexican-American people had been the radio. Because of the proximity to the Mexican border, there was a strong attachment to things Mexican. The music heard in the homes varied with the age groups listening. The older people generally preferred to listen to music that had a ". . . taste of the Revolution or brought back memories of twenty and thirty years ago."[36] The younger

-46-

generation had varied tastes extending from the hero-praising, event-telling corrido to the Hispanicized versions of American popular music, or Americanized versions of Mexican and South-American music.

The false, the illogical and the fantastic were still accepted by many Mexicans. This characteristic was found in greater evidence among the older generation. These people were still preyed upon by other Mexicans, and others, whom the more learned people labeled coyotes (a colloquial term denoting a person who takes advantage of the more ignorant).

Home improvements had followed closely the economic status acquired by the working man. Where there had been money to spend, it had usually gone into improvement of home facilities and into the education of the young.

IV. THE CHURCH

The role of the Church had been an important one for the Mexican-Americans in Arizona. Serving first as a teacher and later adding to its charge that of being one of the strong socializing agents, it had helped these people acquire some of the necessary prestige needed by an immigrant group in a foreign land. As a social outlet the Church tended to increase the rate of acculturation; yet it too had been a factor in spreading the evils of segregation and discrimination.

A popular misconception had been that all Mexicans were Catholic. In an effort to ascertain what percentage of those living in Arizona actually were, questions concerning their church affiliation were included in the survey. The tabulations computed from returned questionnaires indicated that approximately 88 per cent of the Mexican-Americans were Catholic. Of this number, 54 per cent attended church regularly, 12 per cent attended often, and 34 per cent attended occasionally. Of the 88 per cent returned as Catholic, 34 per cent belonged to a religious or church organization.[37]

Segregation. The thorns of segregation and discrimination had not stemmed from the practices of school administrators and employers alone. Segregation for one reason or another had existed in Arizona in many other instances.

Because this investigator was more familiar with the area around Miami, Arizona, the following material is concerned more specifically with the situations as they existed there prior to and including time of completion of this study.

A common sight in Miami until the early 1940's was the sorry spectacle created by three churches all located on the same street. Two of them, facing each other across the main thoroughfare, were of the same denomination. One, the one used by the Anglo-American group, was an impressive concrete structure which boldly displayed the words "Miami Community Presbyterian Church." The other, of lumber construction, with doors that never fully closed and a patchwork pattern of clear and opaque windows, was humbly embellished with the words "Mexican Presbyterian Church." Two blocks west was another lumber shack, leaning slightly to the left and slightly more dilapidated than the second yet proudly proclaiming to the passersby "Colored Baptist Church." Scenes such as this one were not the sole property of Miami; Tucson as well as Phoenix had similar ones.

A bitter thorn created by the practice of segregation had existed in Miami since the early 1920's. Here segregation of the Mexican-American had extended further than the school. In Miami's Catholic church, it was not unusual to see all of the Anglo-Americans sitting on one side of the church while their Mexican-American Catholic brethren sat in their respective area on the opposite side. This conditioned response had its inception during the early 1920's, resulting from the popular misconception that all Mexicans are adept thieves. A Catholic priest of the early 1920's was informed by some of his Anglo-American parishioners that the Mexicans were stealing purses from the pews. Attempting to correct this situation, he directed that henceforth all Mexicans would sit to the right of the altar and all others to the left. This practice had been one of the most difficult obstacles for the Mexican-American group in that area to surmount in their attempts at Americanization. Apparently the stereo-typed cultural definition of the Mexican-Americans was still prevalent and was a major factor contributing to their retarded socialization.

Catholic organizations throughout the state had in late years shown an increase in Mexican-American membership. This in itself indicated a favorable trend in improved relationships between the two groups since some of these same organizations had refused membership to Mexican-Americans in previous years.

Interest in bettering the socio-economic status of the Mexican-Americans took an upward swing during the World War II period, waning somewhat during the post war years. Among the groups that had taken a sincere interest in aiding this group attain better living condition had been some of the church organization which had established missions among the Mexican people in the Phoenix area. Another group which was attempting to develop leaders from within the Mexican-American group itself was the Social Action Department of the National Catholic Welfare Conference, mentioned previously in this study.

The general trend as indicated from an analysis of this chapter was one of increased activity of the Mexican-American group in the social institutions. Although the social barriers had still persisted, education of both the Anglo- and the Mexican-American groups had lessened the load for one and had given understanding to both.

FOOTNOTES

[1] John Gunther, Inside U.S.A. (New York: Harper & Brothers, 1947), p. 910.

[2] J.S. Stocker, "People's Padre," Catholic World, 165:261, June, 1947.

[3] Field notes: Interview with Mr. Roy Yanez, Project Manager, Assistant Housing Director, Phoenix Housing Authority. Phoenix, Arizona, June 14, 1950.

[4] Field notes: Interview with Mr. Roy Yanez.

[5] The U.S. Housing Act, 1937, known as the Wagner-Steagall Act, as amended by the Housing Act of 1949, specifically requires a community to eliminate repair, or close unsafe or unsanitary dwellings substantially equal in number to the number of new dwellings provided by a low-rent project. Source: The Truth about Public Housing, Phoenix Housing Authority report (mimeographed pamphlet), n.p.

[6] Field notes: Interview with Mrs. R. Gallegos, Alianza-Hispano-Americana Fraternal Service Director, Tucson, Arizona, June 27, 1950.

[7] Percentages based on computations from Questionnaire returns. Question 18, Part II. Questionnaire in Appendix.

[8] Percentages based on computations from Questionnaire returned. Question 10, Part III (Questionnaires sent out 75, number returned 50). Questionnaire in Appendix.

[9] Roy C. Rice, "Intergroup Relations in Arizona," Journal of Educational Sociology, 21:244, December, 1947. (Questionnaires sent out 65, number returned 42.)

[10] Percentages based on computations from Questionnaire returns. Question 17, Part II. Questionnaire in Appendix.

[11] Percentages based on computations from Questionnaire returns. Question 16, Part II. Questionnaire in Appendix.

[12] The laws pertaining to segregation of pupils in the public schools of Arizona are to be found under three separate statutes. Source: The Arizona Code, 1939, Section 54-416, p. 465; 54-430, p. 475; 54-918, p. 507. General Laws of Arizona Annotated. Vol. IV (Indianapolis: The Bobbs-Merrill Company, 1940.)

[13] Thomas Edwin Farish, History of Arizona (San Francisco, The Filmer Brothers Electrotype Company, 1916), III, p. 124.

[14] Jennie Ellingson, "History of Arizona Schools Until 1876," Arizona Journal of Education, 1:44, June 10, 1910.

[15] Field notes: From interview with Mr. John V. Lassoe, Executive Secretary, Arizona Council for Civic Unity, Phoenix, Arizona, June 28, 1950.

[16] Field notes: Interview with Mr. Ralph Estrada and Mr. Greg Garcia, attorneys. Material from Docket No. 1473; Petition for Preliminary Injunction in the District Court of the United States, District of Arizona. June 6, 1950.

[17] Board of Trustees; Tolleson School District No. 17, Tolleson, Arizona. School Year 1949-1950.

[18] News item in the Arizona Republic, February 21, 1946, p. 7.

[19] Field notes: Interview with Mr. John V. Lassoe. Source: Copy of letter to him from Doctor George I. Sanchez, dated April 28, 1950.

[20] Field notes: Interview with Mr. John V. Lassoe. Source: Copy of Initiative Measure to submitted directly to the Electors. (Proposed amendment to the Constitution of the State of Arizona. Section 54-430, Arizona Code 1939, Annotated.)

[21] Fred G. Homes, "Close the Breach," A Report of the Study of School Segregation in Arizona (Phoenix: Arizona Council for Civic Unity, January 12, 1950), Topic under the Elementary Schools.

[22] Ibid., et passim.

[23] Questionnaire. Question 8, Part II, Questionnaire in Appendix.

[24] From Questionnaire. Question 9, Part II, Questionnaire in Appendix.

[25] Field notes: Interview with Mrs. J. Martinez, Tiger, Arizona, June 12, 1950.

[26] Tucson Council for Civic Unity, "Proceedings of the Conference on Human Relations," (Tucson, Arizona, April 15, 1950), p. 6.

[27] Field notes: Survey Miami area, May, 1950. (Gringo, as used by the Arizona Mexican-Americans, is a colloquial expression which denotes any person, other than Negro or Indian, who is not of Spanish or Mexican descent.)

[28] M. L. Brooks, "Arizona Educational Directory," (Issued under the direction of Superintendent of Public Instruction, Phoenix, Arizona, School Year 1949-1950), 100 pp.

[29] Roy C. Rice, "Intergroup Relations . . ." op. cit.

[30] All figures cited represent close approximations based on tabulations from the Arizona Educational Directory for the years cited.

[31] Field notes: From interview with Mr. Ernesto Munoz, Veterans Administration Contact Officer, Veteran's Hospital, Tucson, Arizona, June 27, 1950.

[32] Percentages computed from Questionnaire returns. Questions 3 and 4, Part II. Questionnaire in Appendix.

[33] Hubert Howe Bancroft, History of Arizona and New Mexico, 1530-1888. The Works of Hubert Howe Bancroft (San Francisco: The History Company Publishers, 1889), p. 379.

[34] Interview with Mrs. Josefina C. Franco, editor of El Sol, Spanish-language newspaper, Phoenix, Arizona, June 29, 1950 (62 S. Third Street, Phoenix).

[35] Field notes: Writer's survey, Miami, Globe, Superior, Glendale, et al., May-June, 1950.

[36]Field note: Interview with Armando Ramirez Saenz, Tucson, Arizona, June 26, 1950.

[37]Percentages computed from Questionnaire returns. Question 1, 2, Part III. Questionnaire in Appendix.

CHAPTER V

SUMMARY AND CONCLUSIONS

I. GENERAL SUMMARY

The present study was based on the sociological precept that intergroup conflicts are a direct result of misconceptions held by the different groups in regard to each others' racial and national origins, cultural traditions and social institutions.

It was the purpose of this study to ascertain the socio-economic status trends of the Mexican-Americans in Arizona through an analysis of the social and economic undercurrents that had helped to establish this group in the retarded socio-economic position they held at the time this study was made.

The objectives sought within the above frame of reference were primarily the formation of an intelligent interpretation and understanding of the statistics concerning the Mexicans and also the development of an interest in improving human relations between the Anglo-Americans and the Mexican-Americans. These were to be accomplished through the presentation of

1. the Mexican people and the motives behind their immigration into the United States and Arizona;

2. the economic opportunities that had been open to them, with the inclusion of a survey of those practices that had tended to retard them both economically and socially;

3. the social barriers and forces that had acted to retard their acculturation or Americanization.

In keeping with the purpose of the study, the objectives sought and the organization of the study, this summary was divided into three major areas: (1) a historical delineation in Chapter I followed by Chapter II, which attempted to present the motives for the immigration of the Mexicans and a brief survey of their population statistics; (2) a portrayal of the economic development of the Mexican-Americans; (3) an overview of the social and cultural institutions of the group.

<u>Summary, Chapters I and II</u>. The Mexican appeared on the Arizona scene during the early days of the Spanish missionary period. The life of the early Mexican settlers in Arizona was a frontier life with all its hardships. The socio-economic status of the Arizona Mexicans during territorial days was very low, primarily as a result of the treatment accorded them. The misconceptions concerning the group's racial origins, physical stamina, lack of ability and social inequality originated during this period. These misconceptions, in turn, produced social and cultural conflicts between the two groups which had lasted until the time of this study.

They came to Arizona in large numbers during the period of mineral and agricultural expansion concentrating in those areas that offered them economic opportunity and cultural ties with their homeland. During the period of early statehood, they were received with open arms as an economic-commodity only to be later treated with disdain and ostracized during the period of economic depression in this country.

A brief account of the Mexican migratory workers was included in this study. Although this group was not a permanent segment of the total population, their labor and the treatment they received were reflected in the treatment and conditions of the state's native Mexican-Americans.

<u>Summary, Chapter III</u>. The second major area of this study attempted to portray the obstacles encountered by both the immigrant group and their descendants in their attempt to gain economic security. The outstanding obstacles were (1) the limitation of opportunity for economic advancement, (2) the stereotyping of the individuals into narrow occupational and industrial categories, (3) the lack of adequate leadership from and organization in its own ranks to combat the above practices and (4) the inadequate facilities or opportunities to enter the skilled trades as apprentices.

Prior to World War II Mexican-American labor had little labor union representation. The rise in the cost of living that accompanied the war caused the Mexican-American laborers to seek higher wages; the arbitration powers offered by the organized labor unions for securing these wages attracted them and in turn the labor organizations grew in size, becoming a strong factor in procuring better wages and better working conditions for all the workers in general. The mining companies, some of whose total labor personnel was composed of from 50 to 80 per cent Mexican-Americans, were hailed into court on charges of practicing job discrimination; the decisions of the courts favored the workers.

Skilled craftsmen from among the Mexican-American group were very few in number. Poorly represented in the urban areas, they were only slightly better represented in the mining districts of the state.

Occupational opportunities were most limited in the professional areas. Less than 0.1 per cent of the professional people in Arizona were Mexican-Americans, yet Mexican-Americans represented approximately 30 per cent of the population.

Summary, Chapter IV. The third area of investigation in this study was that of social aspects and social institutions. In this chapter the attempt was made to convey, through a description of housing conditions, educational opportunities and limitations, cultural traditions and aspects of the social institutions, a concept of the factors responsible for the slow rate of acculturation, or Americanization, of the Mexican-American minority.

Viewed generally, the housing conditions of the Mexican-Americans in Arizona were deplorable. Blighted areas existed in all sectors of the state. The consoling feature was that some company-owned homes furnished the people with the facilities necessary for sanitary living. Another feature of importance in the Phoenix area was the continued expansion of the housing program initiated in 1941 by Father Emmett McLaughlin. The substandard dwellings in other areas, including the Phoenix suburbs and Tucson, were so abysmally deplorable that Federal, civic and social groups were conducting surveys to determine what improvements could be made.

Segregation and discrimination were still widely practiced in the state's public school systems. Proceedings to eliminate the practices of segregation because of race, color or creed were being considered by the United States District Court of Arizona. The pleadings of the school administrators were that neither segregation nor discrimination were being practiced, but rather separation on the basis of the lack of English proficiency on the part of the Mexican-American children and the accompanying retardation of the English-speaking. Those representing the Mexican-American people contended that the facilities provided the Mexican-American children in their segregated school were below standard on all counts.

Professional placement of teachers of Mexican-American descent was limited in all areas. A comparison of numbers indicated that less than 1.5 per cent of the teachers in Arizona were Spanish-name individuals. An obvious need existed for more teachers from this group.

The home and its cultural traditions had undergone a very small change. The language was still predominantly Spanish. The greatest change had come in the forms of recreation in which the family particpated. Spanish-language papers and periodicals were as much in evidence in the homes as was the influence of Spanish-language radio programs, two factors which had aided in slowing up the Americanization of the group. The superstitious beliefs and myths were still present, but these existed to a greater extent among the older people. Education and acculturation had made some inroads into the thinking and reasoning of the younger generations.

The Church played an important role in the development of the Mexican-American group, although some had derived profit from its socializing influence, others had suffered from its shortcomings. The popular notion that all Mexican were Catholics was proven erroneous. Catholics represented approximately 88 per cent of the total group reporting. The shortcomings of religion had produced in Arizona the not uncommon sight of nationalize religious groups, i.e., "Mexican-Methodist," "Mexican-Presbyterian" and other combined-name churches.

II. CONCLUSIONS

This study, primarily a survey of the socio-economic status trends of the Mexican-Americans in Arizona, made no pretense at analyzing every phase possible in a sociological study of this nature. The limitations imposed by scarcity of reliable data and materials presented the greatest obstacles to the total treatment of this study. Notwithstanding these handicaps, there were certain conclusions derived from the study in conformity with the terms of the problem and its objectives. These were the following:

1. Immigration from Mexico had been largely checked. The tendency was toward a controlled, short-run, labor migration rather than the more permanent type that took place during the 1900 to 1930 period.

2. The native-born Mexican-American population was increasing in a ratio approximating that Anglo-American population of the state.

3. Although some of the misconceptions regarding racial and national origin, cultural traditions, intellectual and technical ability had been eliminated to some degree, they were still strongly in evidence at the time this study was made.

4. The socio-economic status of the Mexican-Americans in Arizona had improved slightly. The improvement was the result of (a) labor union representation, which had eliminated some of the discrimination practiced by employers, (b) the fact that more of the Mexican-Americans were entering the semi-skilled trades and were becoming small business owners, (c) the fact that more Mexican-American children were completing elementary and high school, and (d) the fact that the social institutions were contributing more toward the accommodation and acculturation of the group.

5. The Mexican-Americans in Arizona had been retarded socially and economically as a result of the infringement on their right to equal educational facilities and their right to equal opportunities for employment. This infringement on their rights had produced, in turn, many of the intergroup frictions and conflicts that had existed in Arizona between the Mexican-American minority group and the Anglo-American majority group.

BIBLIOGRAPHY

A. BIBLIOGRAPHIES

Apperson, Evelyn. Mexican-Americans: A Selected Bibliography. Bibliographic
Series No. 7, Chicago: American Council on Race Relations, 1949.

Whittenburg, Clarice T., and George I. Sanchez. Materials Relating to the Education of Spanish-Speaking People, A Bibliography. Inter-American Education Occasional Papers II, Austin: University of Texas Press, February, 1948.

B. BOOKS

del Vayo, J. Alvarez. The Last Optimist. New York: The Viking press, 1950, 406 pp.

Ferguson, Eran. Our Southwest. New York: A.A. Knopf, 1940, 396 pp.

Gamio, Manuel. Mexican Immigration to the United States: A Study of Human Migration and Adjustment. Chicago: University of Chicago Press, 1930, 262 pp.

Griffith, Beatrice Winston. American Me. Boston: Houghton, Mifflin Co., 1948,
341 pp.

Gunther, John. Inside U.S.A. New York: Harper & Brothers, 1947, 979 pp.

McWilliams, Carey. Brothers Under the Skin. Boston: Little Brown and Co.,
1944, 325 pp.

Mowry, Silvester. Arizona and Sonora: The Geography, History, and Resources
of the Silver Region of North America. Third Edition; New York: Harper
& Brothers, 1946, 251 pp.

Tuck, Ruth D. Not With the Fist: Mexican Americans in a Southwest City. New
York: Harcourt, Brace and Co., 1946, 234 pp.

C. PARTS OF SERIES

Arizona Code 1939. General Laws of Arizona Annotated. Vol. IV, 6 vols.; Indianapolis: The Bobbs-Merrill Co., 1940, pp. 465, 475, 507.

Bancroft, Hubert Howe. History of Arizona and New Mexico, 1530-1888. The Works
of Hubert Howe Bancroft. Vol. XVII, 39 vols.; San Francisco: The History
Co. Publishers, 1889, pp. 379, 607, 617.

Farish, Thomas Edwin. History of Arizona. Vol. III (1916), 9 vols.; San Francisco: The Filmer Brothers Electrotype Co., 1915-20, pp. 124, 154.

McWilliams, Carey. North from Mexico, the Spanish-Speaking People of the United States. Louis Adamic, editor, The Peoples of America Series; Philadelphia: J.B. Lippincott Co., 1949, 324 pp.

Steinberg, S.H., editor. "Arizona," The Stateman's Yearbook 1949. New York: The McMillan Co., 1949, p. 576.

United States Bureau of the Census, Sixteenth Census of the United States. Characteristics of the Population. Vol. II, Part 1; Washington, D.C.: United States Department of Commerce, 1940 United States Summary, p. 9.

_____, Fifteenth Census of the United States. Population. Vol. III, Part 1; Washington, D.C.: United States Department of Commerce, 1930 United States Census, p. 1.

D. PERIODICALS

Davis, Kingsley, and Clarence Senior. "Immigration from the Western Hemisphere," Department of Justice Immigration and Naturalization Service, 7:31-39, September, 1949.

Eckerson, Helen F., and Nick D. Collaer. "Border Patrol," Department of Justice Immigration and Naturalization Service, 7:59, November, 1949.

Ellingson, Jennie. "History of Arizona Schools Until 1876," Arizona Journal of Education, 1:42-47, June 10, 1910.

"New Census Returns and Education of Our Spanish-Speaking Population," Education for Victory, 1:7-8, July 15, 1942.

Rice, Roy C. "Intergroup Relations in Arizona," The Journal of Educational Sociology, 21:243-49, December, 1947.

Scully, Michael. "New Life in Old Mexico," Reader's Digest, 48:45-48, February, 1946.

Stocker, J.S., "People's Padre," Catholic World, 165:260-64, June, 1947.

E. MONOGRAPHS, BULLETINS AND PAMPHLETS

Brooks, M.L. "Arizona Educational Directory," Issued under the Direction of Superintendent of Public Instruction, Phoenix, Arizona. School Year 1949-1950, 100 pp.

Case, C.O. "Arizona Educational Directory," Issued under the Direction of: Superintendent of Public Instruction, Phoenix, Arizona. School Year 1914-1915, 93 pp.

Castaneda, Carlos E. "Statement Before the Senate Committee on Labor and Education in the Hearings held September 8, 1944, on Senate Bill 2048," Special Assistant to the President's Committee on Fair Employment Practice. Mimeographed. Washington, D.C., 8 pp.

Galaraza, Ernesto. "Mexican-United States Labor Relations and Problems," Summarized Proceedings III, Fourth Regional Conference, Southwest Council on Education of the Spanish-Speaking People. Albuquerque, New Mexico: Mimeographed, January 23-25, 1950, 5 pp.

Holmes, Fred G. "Close the Breach," A Report of the Study of School Segregation in Arizona. Phoenix: Arizona Council for Civic Unity, January 12, 1950, 16 pp.

Housing Authority of the City of Phoenix. "The Truth About Public Housing," A Housing Authority Report. Phoenix: Housing and Home Finance Agency, Public Housing Administration. Mimeographed Report, 1950, 8 pp.

Lenroot, Katherine F. "The Children's Bureau and Problems of the Spanish-Speaking Minority Group," Washington, D.C.: United States Department of Labor, Children's Bureau, April, 1943, 16 pp.

Lucey, Most Reverend Robert E., S.T.D. "The Spanish Speaking of the Southwest and West," Report on the Conference of Leaders, Washington, D.C.: Social Action Department, National Catholic Welfare Conference, 1943, 44 pp.

Rugg, Earl U. "Intergroup Relations," Final Report, 1946-1949. Greeley Committee, College Study on Intergroup Relations. Greeley, Colorado: Colorado State College of Education, April, 1949, 195 pp.

Sanchez, George I. "First Regional Conference on the Education of Spanish-Speaking People in the Southwest, A Report," Inter-American Education, Occasional Papers Series I. Austin: University of Texas Press, March, 1946, 22 pp.

Saunders, Lyle. "The Spanish-Speaking Population of Texas," Inter-American Education, Occasional Papers V. Austin: University of Texas Press, December, 1949, 56 pp.

Society for Curriculum Study. "Our Minority Groups: Spanish-Speaking People," Building America, Vol. VIII, No. 5. New York: Americana Corporation, 159 pp.

Toledano, Lombardo V. "Judios y mexicanos razas inferiores?" Universidad
    Obrera de Mexico. Mexico, 1942, 34 pp.

Tucson Council for Civic Unity. "Proceedings of the Conference on Human Rela-
    tions." Tucson, Arizona, April 15, 1950, 12 pp.

United States Department of Justice. "Annual Report of the Immigration and
    Naturalization Service, Fiscal Year Ended June 30, 1948." Washington,
    D.C.: United States Department of Justice Publication, 1948, Table 4.

F. UNPUBLISHED THESIS

Baker, Eileen Trimble. "A Source Unit on the Republic of Mexico." Unpublished
    Master's thesis, Arizona State College at Tempe, Arizona, 1948, 103 pp.

Munoz, Rosalio Florian. "The Relation of Bilingualism to Verbal Intelligence and
    Social Adjustment Among Mexican Children in the Salt River Valley, Ari-
    zona." Unpublished Master's thesis, Arizona State Teachers College,
    Tempe, Arizona, 1938, 81 pp.

G. FIELD NOTES

Interviews and notations from the following sources:

Baca, Jose R. President United Steelworkers of America CIO, Phoenix, Arizona.

Castro, Raul. Attorney, Tucson, Arizona.

Estrada, Ralph. Attorney, Phoenix, Arizona.

Franco, Jesus (Sr.,). Mexican Consul, Phoenix, Arizona.

Franco, Josefina C. (Sra.). Editor of El Sol, Phoenix, Arizona.

Gallegos R. (Mrs.). Fraternal Service Director, Alianza-Hispano-Americana,
    Tucson, Arizona.

Interviews with Labor representatives in Phoenix. AFL and CIO Unions, June, 1950.

Investigator's Survey; Globe, Miami, Superior, Phoenix, Tucson, Tempe and others.
    May-July, 1950.

Lassoe, John V. Executive Secretary, The Greater Phoenix Council for Civic Unity,
    Phoenix, Arizona.

Manzo, Genaro. Accountant, Jacome's, Tucson, Arizona.

Martinez, J. (Mrs.). President, Altar Society, Tiger, Arizona.

Morales, Carlos. Member Counseling Board, The Greater Phoenix Council for Civic Unity, Phoenix, Arizona.

Munoz, Ernesto. Veterans Administration, Contact Officer, Tucson, Arizona.

Saenz, Armando Ramirez. Radio repairman, Tucson, Arizona.

Smith, Placida G. (Mrs.). Executive Director, Phoenix Friendly House.

Vasquez, Ocelio. Agricultural Employment Assistant of the United States Employment Service, Phoenix, Arizona.

Yanez, Roy. Assistant Housing Director, Housing Authority of the City of Phoenix, Arizona.

H. NEWSPAPERS

Arizona Daily Star (Tucson, June 5, 1950.

Arizona Labor Journal, A.F.L., March, 1949.

The Arizona Republic (Phoenix), February 21, 1946.

Voces, La Revista del Noroeste (Ciudad Obregon, Sonora), Vol. V, Nos. 40-47, April-August, 1949.

APPENDIX

APPENDIX A

COPY OF LETTER ACCOMPANYING QUESTIONNAIRE

June 17, 1950

The purpose of this surfey is to ascertain the socio-economic status trends of the people of Arizona who are commonly referred to as "Mexican" or Spanish".

Your response will aid us greatly in the compiling of this data for presentation as a thesis. All the material returned shall be treated in a strictly professional manner.

The questionnaire which has been compiled requires from fifteen to thirty minutes to answer. We hope you will accept our invitation to fill out this form in order that the information for the entire state may be complete.

Because the material returned must be analyzed and compiled before June 26, we would appreciate your filling out this form immediately upon receiving it. Enclosed is a stamped, self-addressed envelope for your convenience in returning the questionnaire.

Thank you for your cooperation.

Sincerely yours,

Raymond J. Flores, B.A.
Graduate Student

RJF:irp

SURVEY QUESTIONNAIRE

Subject: The Socio-Economic Status of Arizona Mexicans.

We are greatly in need of a simple inventory form from which we can make a report indicating the social and economic status of the "Mexican-American" people of this state.

By "socio-economic status," we mean the position an individual or a family occupies with reference to prevailing average standards of cultural possessions, effective income, material possessions, and participation in the group activities of the community.

No name of an individual or family is wanted. Information which does mention names, as well as all other information, will be treated in a professional manner. Please feel free to say as much as you like and whatever you like on any question.

PART I.   PERSONAL INVENTORY

1. Town in which you are living _____ County _____

2. Are you a native of Arizona?_____If not, where were you born?_____
   Citizen? Yes___ No___

3. Are you married?_____

4. How many dependents do you have?_____

5. What approximately is your annual salary?_____

6. What approximately was it ten years ago?_____

7. What approximately was it in 1930_____1920_____1910_____

8. If you were not earning a salary for those years, what approximately was
   your father's salary for 1930_____ 1920_____ 1910_____

(Note: These figures will represent the growth in earning power if any existed.)

PART II. FAMILY INVENTORY

1. When did your antecedents come from Mexico? Year_____

2. If your parents came from Mexico, did they leave for:

	Yes	No
a. Religious reasons	____	____
b. Economic reasons	____	____
c. Both	____	____

   d. Other _____

   _____

3. Did your parents speak English?_____

4. Do you speak Spanish at home?_____English?_____Both?_____

5. What year in school (American) did your parents complete? (Circle one.)

   Father: 1 2 3 4 5 6 7 8 9 10 11 12 - College: 1 2 3 4 5

   Mother: 1 2 3 4 5 6 7 8 9 10 11 12 - College: 1 2 3 4 5

   If parents attended school in Mexico, indicate here approximate level attained.
   1 2 3 4 5 6 7 8 9 10 11 12 Other_____

6. What grade did you complete? (Circle one.) 1 2 3 4 5 6 7 8 9 10 11 12
   College: 1 2 3 4 5 Underline to indicate level wife attained.

7. Did you attend a segregated school for "Mexicans"? Yes_____ No_____

8. Are your children attending a segregated school? Yes_____No_____

9. In a short statement give the reason the school administrators give for practicing segregation, if it exists in your community. (If more room is needed, use back of sheet.)

10. What type of work did your first antecedent from Mexico do when he came to the United States?_____ Approximately salary_____

11. What type of work do you do?_____

    Number of employees you supervise_____

12. If any of your children are over 18, and they hold a job, what type of work is it? _____

_____

_____

13. Do you own or rent the house you live in? (Indicate which.) _____

14. Do you own an automobile or a truck? Make_____ Year 19_____ Model_____

15. Do you have a radio?_____ Television set?_____ Piano?_____

16. Does your house have a shower?_____ Tub?_____ Inside toilet?_____

17. Do you own a refrigerator?_____ Electric or gas range?_____

18. What type of homes predominate in the neighborhood you live in? (Check which.) Brick_____ Concrete_____ Stucco frame_____ Wood frame _____ Other_____

19. What is the estimated value of real estate (property) in your district?_____

PART III. COMMUNITY RELATIONS

1. Church Preference_____ Attend regularly_____ Often_____
   Occasionally_____ Never_____

2. Do you belong to any religious organizations? Name._____

3. Are you, or any of your family, members of civic organizations?_____
   Fraternal organizations_____ Insurance groups_____
   Other_____

4. What office do you hold?_____ Have held_____

5. How many people of Mexican descent hold public offices in your community?
   Appointed_____ Elected_____ High School Teachers_____
   Elementary school teachers_____ Other_____
   (If exact numbers are unknown, approximate number will do.)

6. Has the Mexican community of your town ever been forbidden from participation in events at local places of amusement, such as: Dances_____ Swimming Pools_____ Restaurants_____ Other_____
   (Indicate whether "Spanish Night" is still practiced.)

7. What action has been taken to eliminate this practice of segregation or discrimination? (A brief statement will do. If you know of actual cases of such practices, and of the people involved, we would appreciate the names, if obtainable. The material will be treated professionally. Please use the back of this sheet for answer.)

8. When with a group of other persons of Mexican descent, do you call yourself
   - Mexican?_____ "Raza"?_____ Spanish?_____ Other?_____

9. When with a group of "Anglo" or "Non-Mexican" persons, do you refer to yourself as: Mexican_____ Spanish _____ Spanish-speaking_____
   Latin-American_____ Spanish-American_____ Other_____

10. Do the people in your district live in distinctive areas_____ or do they mix?_____. (Indicate predominant characteristic.)

11. Are inter-group problems in your district likely to improve in the next few years_____ or grow worse_____ or remain the same?_____
    Tell why you believe so.

12. Will you please state here your reaction to this inquiry; whether the questions were of value and interest; whether other questions should have been asked (state questions.) Your criticisms and any additional information you may want us to know.